Trees
for fruit and foliage

Stirling Macoboy

Tr

For the United Nations
International Year of the Tree, 1982-83

ees for fruit and foliage

Lansdowne Press
Sydney Auckland London New York

Published by Lansdowne Press, Sydney
a division of RPLA Pty Limited
176 South Creek Road, Dee Why West, N.S.W.,
Australia, 2099
First published 1982
Reprinted 1986
© Copyright Stirling Macoboy 1982
Produced in Australia by the publisher
Typeset in Australia by V.I.P. Typesetters
Printed in Hong Kong
by South China Printing Co.

Designed by Jim Paton
Edited by Sue Wagner

**National Library of Australia
Cataloguing-in-Publication Data**
Macoboy, Stirling, 1927-,
Trees for fruit and foliage.
Includes index.
ISBN 0 7018 1625 2.
1. Fruit trees. 2. Fruit-culture. I. Title.
634

PHOTOGRAPHS

Title Page: Red Maple, *Acer rubrum Tridens* in
New Hampshire.
Opposite Page: 'Setting the woods on fire' —
autumn colour in New England

All photographs by the author except
Adansonia gregorii, page 19, by Reg Morrison,
Pistacia vera, page 110, by Tess Mallos.

ACKNOWLEDGEMENTS

The trees in this book were photographed
In Australia
At Brisbane Botanic Gardens, New Farm Park,
Mt Tamborine and Cumbabah, Qld; The National
Botanic Garden and Lanyon, ACT; Derby, W.A.;
Blackburn, Burwood, Maryborough and
Melbourne, Vic; Armidale, Bathurst, Bellingen,
Botany Bay, Bowral, Carlingford, Centennial
Park, Charlotte Pass, Cooma, Epping,
Glenbrook, Goulburn, Lane Cove, Leura,
Mittagong, Mosman, Mt Canobolas, Mt Irvine,
Narrabeen Lakes, Narwee, Neutral Bay,
Northbridge, Orange, Port Macquarie, Royal
Botanic Gardens (Sydney), St Ives, Stony Range
Reserve, Turramurra, Umeralla, Willoughby and
Yowie Bay, all in N.S.W.
In the United States
At Arnold Arboretum, Concord and Lexington,
Mass; Mystic and the University of Connecticut,
Conn; Mohonk and New York City, N.Y.; Foster
Gardens, the Honolulu Academy of Arts, Iolani
Palace, Lyon Arboretum, Moana Lua Park,
Queens Hospital and University of Hawaii, in
Hawaii; Bel Air, Beverly Hills, Descanso
Gardens, Hollywood, La Brea Park, Los Angeles
State and County Arboretum, Pasadena, Rancho
Santa Ana, San Marino, Strybing Arboretum,
UCLA Botanic Garden, UCLA Japanese Garden,
all in California.
In Europe
Bagatelle, Jardin des Plantes, Malmaison and
Palais Luxembourg in Paris; Prague Botanic
Garden, Pruhonice and the US Embassy,
Prague; Bantry Bay and Garinish, Ireland; Hillier
Arboretum, Kew Gardens, and RHS Garden,
Wisley, U.K.; and in Greece.
In Asia
Makiling and the University of the Philippines,
Philippine Republic; Meiji Shrine, Shinjuku Go-en
and Tokyo Botanic Garden, Tokyo; Ching Chung
Koon Temple, Hong Kong Botanic Garden,
Kadoorie Farm and Repulse Bay Hotel, Hong
Kong; and at Macao.
In the Pacific
Hotels Ariana, Taaone, and Tahara'a in Tahiti;
Bora Bora, Moorea, Ra'iatea and Tahaa, all in
French Polynesia; American Samoa; Rarotonga,
Cook Islands.
My thanks to the unknown gardeners at whose
homes many of the best trees were found, and to
the many garden-minded friends who brought
individual trees to my attention, and who helped
with the transport and notetaking.

CONTENTS

INTRODUCTION

All trees are beautiful in the wild, but when a garden has room for but a few, we must take care to choose those which will return value in proportion to their size. There's no sense in planting a giant if it's going to interfere with overhead power lines or require constant lopping to keep it within bounds, so that it becomes only a parody of its natural shape.

Shade, shelter and privacy are of course important — but almost any tree can provide those in an average small garden. Let us rather look for species which have a particular beauty of foliage — whether in shape or colour of the leaves, brilliant hues of new growth in spring or at leaf-fall in autumn — so that the tree becomes an integral part of our garden display.

Those trees which are grown particularly for their flowering beauty are covered in a companion volume, **Trees for Flower and Fragrance.** But there are many others in which the transient flower display (lovely though it is) takes second place to the beauty of foliage and/or a decorative display of fruits. These fruits (for botanically speaking they are all fruits) may consist of acorns, beans, berries, cones, drupes, nuts, pomes and many other subclassifications. They are of course basically the tree's method of reproduction, for they contain the seeds from which new trees will grow. But nature has cleverly designed them to appeal to the appetites of many diverse creatures which will help spread the seed and ensure the continuity of the tree species. Some fruits will appeal to birds only, others to reptiles or small tree-dwelling mammals, the great majority of them to the creature with the most omnivorous appetite of all — man!

This book not only shows a vast range of trees that produce magnificent fruit and foliage when planted in the right climate. The accompanying text describes what climate that is, the position the tree likes, its size and season of growth. You'll learn how to plant it, how to prune it, how to care for it.

The choice is wide, wherever you live, and we hope this book will help you make it.

Silver Maple — *Acer saccharinum* ▶

PLANT A TREE — HELP SAVE A WORLD!

Since time immemorial, trees have been the most prominent living feature of any natural setting away from the polar regions of the earth. They are the backbone of life as we know it, for they conserve water, control pollution, protect the very earth itself. They are the oxygen banks, the air cleaners, the rainbringers and erosion preventers of nature. They are also her most beautiful creation.

Almost every aspect of our life is in some way influenced by trees. They bring us shade, shelter and privacy; their wood builds our houses, our bridges and boats. Their fruits help feed and furnish and comfort us; their dead tissue has been transformed over the ages into the fossil fuels of coal and gas and oil that keep the wheels of industry turning, grant us the blessings of fire and warmth, make it possible for us to be transported in comfort by land, by sea, by air. Trees supply us indirectly with everything in life, yet for generations we have cut them down without replacement, without a thought for the future that seems so far off, yet is so dangerously close.

Already, entire regions have been denuded of their natural forests, and the resulting atmospheric pollution of carbon dioxide (which trees would have converted into life-giving oxygen) is causing great concern. Scientists believe this is causing dangerous changes in the world climate which could ultimately spell out the end of man's reign on earth.

If we are tree lovers as we claim, we must replant now, and continually, to help redress the damage already done to our soil, our climate, our wild life, our entire ecology. For what chance does a single tree (or even a whole race of trees) stand, when measured against the apathy of politicians, the greed of land developers, the short-sightedness of farmers?

Each and every one of us must speak out *now* for the protection and replacement of the trees that were once around us. The trees without which our civilization could never have risen to its present heights — and without which it certainly has no future.

Neutral Bay, N.S.W.
March 1982

TREES FOR FRUIT AND FOLIAGE — HOW TO GROW THEM

Whichever tree you've chosen to beautify and enrich your garden, and wherever you decide to place it, correct planting and maintenance will guarantee swift, even growth and a long, colourful span of years.

WHEN TO PLANT A TREE

Modern nursery practice is to sell all young trees ready-growing in containers, so they can be planted out any time of year without risk of loss. They will, however, grow faster, with minimum transplant shock, if certain basic rules are followed. Completely deciduous trees are best set out in late winter or very early spring, when bare and dormant. Evergreen trees from cold or temperate climates do best when planted in mid-autumn so the roots have time to get established before cold weather halts growth, or in mid-spring with the sap in full flow and a full season's growth ahead of them. The main exceptions are trees from distinctly tropical climates which are customarily planted in warm (even hot) weather, with appropriate care and water so they do not dehydrate.

Ornamental trees for garden use are expensive items — you are paying not only for the tree itself, but for the time and labour incurred in raising it to a suitable size for sale — generally at three or four years of age. Therefore it makes sense to take every possible precaution to ensure its healthy survival.

TESTING FOR DRAINAGE AND DEPTH

The most common cause of failure is incorrect drainage. If water remains around the tree's roots, it will drown. Test the chosen position by digging a hole at least 30cm/12in deep and fill it with water. If water remains in the hole more than 12 hours, you'll need to improve the drainage. This is done by redigging the hole at least 30cm deeper than the young tree's roots will require, and filling in the extra depth with gravel, crushed tile or other draining material. If your pre-planting excavation reveals solid rock less than 50cm/20in below the surface, you'd better choose another planting site. A mature tree's roots need to go way down to support it against wind and supply it with moisture in periods of excessive dryness. When this is the only *possible* position for the tree, however, the difficulty can be overcome by constructing a raised bed with retaining wall to provide the necessary depth of soil.

PREPARING FOR PLANTING

Having decided on a suitable position, dig a hole at least twice the width of the root-ball in the container, and at least 30cm deeper. Professional gardeners would say, the poorer the natural soil, the wider and deeper your hole should be. If you're planting in a lawn, mark out a neat circle about 1m/3ft in diameter, then cut and lift out the circumscribed grass area. Set the grass aside for later use. Lay a sheet of plastic on the

PLANTING A TREE

a: Dig hole, place stake off-centre, partly refill.

b: Place tree at correct level, then refill hole.

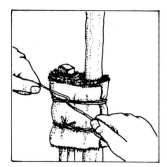
c: Water, then tie trunk to stake, as shown.

8

lawn nearby, and dig all soil from the hole onto it, until you have reached an adequate depth. Loosen the soil in the bottom of the hole with a garden fork to help drainage.

Now insert a heavy garden stake (treated with preservative) slightly off-centre in the hole and hammer well in. The stake should reach at least 1m above soil level, or to the lower branches in the case of a taller tree. Chop up the removed grass-turf and place it around the stake, grass-side down. Mix the removed soil thoroughly with garden compost and sand, and partly fill the hole so the young tree's rootball will be on a level with the surrounding area. Tread the filling firmly so that it is reasonably level.

PLANTING THE TREE

Now, having watered the young tree in its container, place it in position. Do not risk root damage by pulling the tree out of the container. Cut it away with secateurs if plastic, with tin snips if metal. Be sure you finally slide the container base away from under the plant. The whole root ball should now be visible, the tree's container soil level with the surrounding area, or slightly above it. If roots are wound around the perimeter of the ball, they should be gently teased out with a hand fork, and spread radially out across the hole. Add more soil mixture until the hole is three-quarters full; pack down lightly with your foot to get rid of air pockets. Scatter a couple of handfuls of slow-release fertilizer (bone meal is ideal) over the covered root area, then a layer of compost or moistened peat. Add several buckets of water at this time to help settle the soil around the roots. Turn in the balance of the enriched soil — but this time do not tamp. Rake it level, leaving a slight depression away from the trunk to collect water.

Soak the newly planted tree slowly and deeply. Finally, tie the tree firmly to the stake in one or more places. Use a soft material such as hessian or burlap strips that will not cut into the bark. This should first be wound around the stake several times so stake and tree cannot rub together. When several layers thick, the whole can be secured with garden twine or wire. Alternatively, you can buy a proprietary tree tie, which is easier to loosen or remove as the trunk thickens.

If the tree comes already balled in burlap or hessian, place it in position on top of a slight mound in the hole, loosen the ties and leave the burlap in place when you fill in the hole. Roots will grow right through and it will soon rot away. If the tree is balled in plastic, however, this must be completely removed. Balled trees are best supported by guy-wires to prevent their rocking in the wind and loosening young roots. Run the wires through small sections of rubber or plastic hose looped around the trunk and stretch each of them taut to small stakes hammered firmly in around the tree. Three should be enough, at regular spacing.

AFTER CARE FOR NEW TREES

Keep the cleared lawn area around the newly planted tree free of weeds and grass for several years at least, and mulch to a depth of at least 10cm/4in before the hot weather begins in late spring. This will help retain moisture and keep the roots cool. The mulch could be shredded pine bark, lawn clippings, apricot hulls, peat or whatever is commonly available in your area.

The young tree will need regular water at least twice a month for the first two years — the dryness of the soil being the key to fre-

LOPPING A BRANCH

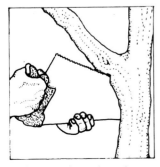

d: *Partly undercut branch, 20cm/8in out from trunk.*

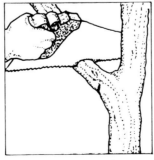

e: *Saw through from above, 10cm/4in beyond first cut.*

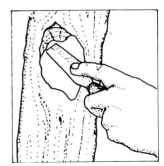

f: *Remove stub flush and paint with tree-wound paint.*

quency. A slow dribbler hose is best, spread around the root area to correspond with the spread of the branches at any time.

Check the ties attaching the tree to the supporting stake in late spring and summer. If they seem tight, loosen them off. It should be possible to remove them, together with the stake, at the end of two years.

FEEDING THE TREE

Young trees need little or no feeding beyond what they pick up from the surrounding mulch. After several years, however, a regular feeding will be beneficial. In the case of foliage trees this will normally be in spring; for fruiting species often twice or more a year. It is customary to feed heavy-fruiting citrus varieties at least 500 grammes/1 pound of poultry manure or citrus fertilizer for *each year of the tree's growth,* twice a year. Again, the important area is well out from the trunk beneath the perimeter of the branches. That's where the feeding roots are. Make a number of holes 20cm/8in deep over the root area using a crowbar or similar pointed tool. Through a funnel, half-fill the holes with a fertilizer specially formulated for shrub and tree growth. Top up the holes with soil, and water deeply.

PRUNING THE TREE

Trees should not be over-pruned: after all, they grow to a shape set by nature. Provided you have chosen a tree that will not outgrow its allotted space, the only reasons for pruning should be (a) to help it get established; (b) to ensure healthy, even growth; (c) to improve yield of fruit or flowers by encouraging the development of multiple flowering twigs. A tree's root mass is usually equivalent to the mass of its branches and foliage. The foliage can therefore evaporate moisture as quickly as the roots can soak it up. If there has been any loss or damage to roots at the time of planting, it is essential to trim the young branches to help balance the loss. Trim your tree, in any case, before new growth starts, forcing the sap to flow in the direction you have chosen. Cut cleanly, with sharp secateurs, any damaged or dead wood, any crossing twigs that may rub, damaging the bark. Trim away young shoots to the height you envisage as exposed trunk (within the first metre initially, to a greater height later on). If thinning out branches, give preference to one of two either directly opposite one another at the same height, or directly above one another on the same side of the tree. The general idea is to encourage a spread of branches spaced equally at various heights, so that rain and sun can reach all parts. Suckers from below graft level must at all times be removed, preferably by tearing them away.

Pruning or lopping of branches too large for your secateurs must always be done in this way: first, make a deep cut with a saw on the *underside* of the branch, at least 20cm/8in out from the trunk. Begin a second cut on the top side of the branch, 10cm beyond the first. This time cut right through, and when the branch breaks away, it can strip bark *only* back to the first cut. Finally remove the branch stub parallel with the trunk surface, again cutting from below. This will leave a wound wider than the diameter of the cut branch. Paint or spray the raw surface with an asphalt tree-wound sealer to prevent fungus infection. Within a year or two the bark will grow right over it! Pruning is best done as soon as possible after flower fall.

SEASONAL PROTECTION

In cold climates, where there is regular frost or even snow, the trunks of young trees need protection from frostbite and bark split. This can be assured by wrapping the trunk in strips of burlap at the end of autumn. (The Japanese tie the tree in jackets of bundled straw.) Place a layer of mulch at least 15cm deep over the root area. The same protection (but applied in spring) will protect young trunks and roots from dehydration and sunburn in hot dry areas. Bark is the mature tree's natural protection, but on saplings it is not much thicker than your own skin.

PESTS AND DISEASES

These are generally less troublesome than on smaller plants — but when infestations do occur, they are also more difficult to eradicate due to the tree's bulk and height. Fruiting trees do of course present special problems of their own, notably codling moth in pome fruits (apples, pears etc) and the pesky fruit fly in many areas and countries. For the former, trees must be sprayed with Carbaryl at petal-fall and again regularly at 14 day intervals up to a total of 6 sprayings. All infected fruit must be destroyed by burning.

The fruit fly is even more of a problem in areas to which it has spread. It attacks almost every type of fruit, both on trees and on smaller plants such as tomato and capsicum. The fruit-bearing trees must be saturated with a systemic insecticide such as Rogor beginning 6 weeks before probable harvest date and continuing weekly. Spray not only the fruit, but over and under the foliage as well. Best get a detailed leaflet from your department of agriculture or local nurseryman.

Caterpillars of all kinds can be as destructive as on smaller plants, and the foliage should be sprayed with Malathion or a similar insecticide on a still day. Make sure you wear goggles and a face mask and don't stand on the lee side of any tree you are spraying.

Red spider mite can be a disfiguring pest, especially on ornamental conifers in dry weather. Spray as above and raise humidity by misting foliage and keeping a damp mulch around the tree.

Any other disease problems should be discussed with your local authority. But please, take along a specimen of the diseased foliage or fruit when you pay them a visit. Just as in human diagnosis, the presence of the patient (or part of it) is essential.

HOW TO USE THIS BOOK

All trees included in this book are arranged in the alphabetical order of their botanical names — in some cases, the only names the trees have. These may sometimes be hard to remember, but they have the advantage of being universally understood, which popular names in any modern language are not. If you know the botanical name already, just leaf through the pages until you come to it in alphabetical order. If you know only a popular name, e.g., Chestnut, turn to the comprehensive Index beginning on page 156. Here you will find all commonly used popular names and synonyms, again in alphabetical order, and each popular name will refer you to the plant's botanical name, and to the page on which the entry begins: e.g.,

Chestnut, see *Castanea* 37.

There are many more popular names than botanical names listed because many tree genera have more than one popular name, or include more than one species, each of which has its own popular name.

Altogether, over 430 species of fruiting and foliage trees are listed and described, together with innumerable varieties. Over 300 of these are illustrated in full colour.

Each entry includes a great deal of useful information, some of it in abbreviated form in the heading.

The first line of each entry gives the tree's generic name only, printed in large capital letters: e.g., PRUNUS, the generic name for all apricots, cherries, peaches and plums, whether fruiting or ornamental.

The generic name is followed by one or more popular names: generally, these are the English names for the whole genus, or for its most prominent members. These are printed in normal type.

After this come three more lines in heavy type, each prefixed by an asterisk (*).

The first line, e.g.,

* Deciduous /fast

indicates firstly whether the tree will drop all of its leaves at any one time or whether it is evergreen; a second group of words gives information about the tree's rate of growth to flowering and fruiting maturity — fast, slow or medium.

The second line, e.g.,

* Autumn colour /berries

indicates the tree's principal season of foliage display and the type (and sometimes season) of the fruits it bears.

The third line, e.g.,

* Ht: to 10m /30ft

tells the tree's maximum height in metres and in feet, and will help you decide where to plant it. Often the tree's height in cultivation will be only a fraction of its height in nature — if so, this will be indicated within the text. When more than one species of the particular tree genus is dealt with in the entry, this line will express the group's height as a range, e.g., **Psidium,**

* Ht: 8-10m /25-30ft

More information about height of individual species is given in the body of the text.

Finally, each heading includes a group of symbols (anywhere from 1 to 3). These are in the form of letters enclosed by a square.

C Shows that the tree grows well in cold-winter areas (though it may grow elsewhere in a shaded position).

T Shows that it thrives in any temperate climate (though its range may be wider).

H That the tree does best in a hot climate (tropical to subtropical). Very few tropical trees will flower or fruit in a cold winter climate.

As some trees are quite adaptable, however, the three squared symbols may appear in many different combinations.

Finally, at the right of each heading is a drawing showing the tree's most common shape at maturity (or the shape of its most commonly raised species). These drawings can of necessity be only a very rough guide, except where only one species of the tree is both grown and described. Together with the tree's given height, they will enable you to calculate its probable spread.

Within the entry itself is all sorts of additional information for the home gardener or tree spotter. This includes country or range of origin; methods of propagation; soil requirements; natural pests; minimum winter temperature; ideal position or light intensity; uses in commerce, history and many other things. Generally, shape and appearance of foliage will be described, often with details of bark and fruit as well. There are also descriptions of popular foliage-colour varieties. Though each entry is necessarily brief, you'll find everything you need to know for raising and making best use of a whole world of trees with wonderful fruit and foliage.

ABIES

Fir, Balsam
* **Evergreen/fast**
* **Upward-pointing cones**
* **Ht: to 100m/300ft** [C]

One of the great tree genera of the world (great in stature, great in their importance to man) are the Firs or Balsams, the original Christmas trees of the Northern Hemisphere.

They are survivors from the last ice age, gradually retreating to the mountains of northern Europe, Siberia, Japan and the Rocky Mountains of North America. With the spread of civilization the three dozen species scattered around the cold winter areas of the north are a dying race. Valued for their timber and their rich harvest of perfumed balsam, most Firs literally ooze with this gum which is used in pharmacy and optics, and for the fresh 'woodsy' smell of many toiletries.

In the wild, Firs grow at an astonishing rate — 1m in a year is common — and reach a vast size. Firs of almost 100m have been recorded. Their aptly chosen Latin name **Abies** is from *abeo* — I rise!

Size would rule them out for the average garden, even if they could be persuaded to grow at sea level, or in the polluted air of today's cities, but in the hill country or by the mountain weekender, they make a marvellous specimen tree — tall, straight and with a delightful fragrance.

Firs do in fact come in many shapes and sizes, and at a quick glance greatly resemble many of the other conifers, notably the Spruces (see **Picea**), but there are several details which set them apart. The leaves almost invariably bear two parallel silver lines on the underside; the cones (often colourful when young) point upwards like the candles on a Christmas tree, whereas on the other conifers that are similar in appearance, they hang down.

Apart from those illustrated, more common species include **A. alba,** the European Fir, to 5m; **A. cephalonica,** the Greek Fir, to 35m; **A. concolor,** the Colorado White Fir, to 50m; **A. delavayi** from China, to 30m, violet cones; **A. nordmanniana** from Greece, to 70m.

Abies grow readily from seed contained in the ripened cones.

Abies nobilis
Noble Fir

Abies homolepis
Nikko Fir

Acer saccharum
Sugar Maple

ACER

Maple, Sycamore
* **Deciduous /fast**
* **Autumn colour,
   winged seeds**
* **Ht: 1-35m /3-100ft** C T

By no means the most prolific of tree genera in terms of the number of species (**Acacia** or **Eucalyptus** would each outnumber them by at least six to one), the Maples display the most astonishing range of leaf shapes and coloration. Japanese gardeners alone catalogue hundreds of named varieties.

Native to cool temperate zones of all three continents in the Northern Hemisphere, they have adapted marvellously to cultivation in every part of the world away from the actual tropics, and collectively are probably the most widely planted of specimen trees.

Always with a certain delicacy, Maples come in all shapes and sizes from the low natural bonsai-habit of some dwarf Japanese varieties to the tall, fast-growing Silver and Sugar Maples of North America.

Almost all of them are deciduous, producing a miraculous spectrum of colour as their leaf-chlorophyll changes in autumn. This effect is one of the world's great natural wonders in America's New England states, where an October visit is an experience never to be forgotten. But make your

14

ACER (continued)

schedule flexible — the opening of the big colour show depends on an exact combination of sunny days and frosty nights.

While photographing for this book in Europe, I received a panic call from Boston, Massachusetts, where I had planned to arrive on 21 October. A cold snap had revised all predictions and the colour peak was expected weeks earlier. I arrived on 6 October, and the next day's country drive was a trip in every sense of the word. I was left with senses reeling from an over-indulgence in orange and scarlet, almost drunk with the vintage smell of decaying chlorophyll.

In spite of their wide variety, all Maples have several features in common. First the leaves are sharply toothed (the name **Acer** is Latin for sharp) and generally in some form digitate (resembling a spread hand), though with anything from three to thirteen lobes of varying lengths and complexity. Secondly, after a rather inconspicuous flowering, they bear masses of distinctive boomerang-shaped seeds known as keys. These consist of two seeds or samaras, each with a single wing. The precise angle of the wings to each other is one of the principal means of species identification.

The winged keys can fly quite a distance, as any Maple grower knows.

Acer saccharinum
Silver Maple

Acer campestre
Field Maple

Acer rubrum
Red Maple

15

Acer X 'Schwedleri Nigra'
Crimson King Maple

Acer CV 'Brilliantissimum'
Sycamore Maple

Acer griseum
Paperbark Maple

Acer palmatum
Japanese Maple

Acer opalus
Italian Maple

Acer CV 'Aconitifolium'
Fern-leaf Maple

Acer CV 'Elegans'
Variegated Box Elder

Acmena smithii
Lillypilly

ACMENA

Lillypilly
* **Evergreen /fast**
* **Autumn fruit**
* **Ht: to 8m /24ft** T H

Once upon a time, there was a beautiful race of glossy-leafed trees called **Eugenia,** after the European military leader, Prince Eugene of Savoy. Considered the largest genus of trees in nature, they were related to the Eucalypts and their special attraction was a profusion of showy berries in late summer. In Australia, they were popularly known as Lillypilly.

Today, taxonomists have given many of them different botanical names. Most are now called **Syzygium** (which see), but the old favourite Lillypilly is listed as **Acmena smithii.**

It is a tall, graceful tree, often with branches of a distinctly weeping habit. It originates from eastern Australia, but now grows in California, South Africa, Hawaii and many other places. The leaves are small and shiny, the fruit quite variable from white to mauve and 1cm in diameter.

Acmena enjoys deep, rich soil with the companionship of other plants and plenty of moisture. The white blossoms have no petals, but do have a mass of white stamens, and look quite charming in early summer.

Propagation is from either seed or cuttings, and **Acmena** has been successfully used as a street tree.

ADANSONIA

Baobab, Bottle Tree,
Judas Bag

* **Deciduous /slow**
* **Autumn fruit**
* **Ht: to 13m /40ft** T H

Imagine, if you can, a tree that may develop a trunk up to 10m in diameter, and yet reach its branches no more than 13m in the air! That's the **Adansonia** or Baobab — a native of dry, outback areas of Australia, Africa and Malagasy (Madagascar).

Named for a French botanist called Adanson, these trees live for an amazing length of time (some African specimens have been estimated to be over five thousand years old) and are often the only surviving vegetation for miles in times of drought. This is because the light, fleshy wood consists mostly of hollow chambers which store water from favourable seasons — up to tens of thousands of gallons of it.

No wonder they were actually worshipped in their harsh, natural African environment. A trunk full of water and handsome digitate leaves that make useful cattle fodder in hard times are only its most obvious features. The fibrous bark may be converted into paper, rope or even a rough cloth, and in processing yields a useful gum. The fruit pulp makes a refreshing acid beverage, and the seeds are almost overflowing with medicinal oil.

Adansonias are often called Bottle Trees, and some ancient specimens, hollowed out by termites, have been used as jails, storage houses or even burial chambers!

Obviously not a likely choice for the home garden, the grotesque, almost ugly **Adansonias** are such curiosities that they are often planted in botanic gardens as a tourist attraction.

They are deciduous, and in a dry year may not produce leaves at all. But generally, the leaves are preceded by 10cm white flowers with reflexed petals. These open on long, hanging stems, and are followed by velvety, cylindrical fruit up to 42cm in length. (The appearance of these has led to one of the Baobab's more gruesome popular names — Dead Rat Tree.) As noted above, however, they are quite edible.

Judas Bag is another popular name, likening the fruit to an ancient purse used to hold silver coins.

Adansonia digitata
Dead Rat Tree

Adansonia gregorii
Baobab

AGATHIS

Kauri, Tennis-ball Tree
* **Evergreen/slow**
* **Spectacular cones**
* **Ht: 25-50m/75-150ft** T H

Scattered here and there about the Pacific, the lofty **Agathis** or Kauris are Southern Hemisphere conifers, but not your ordinary needle-covered, Christmas-tree type of conifer. The very name **Agathis** marks their first unusual point. It is Greek for a ball of string and that's exactly what the large fruit or cones look like — a grey ball of string or, according to the Hawaiians, a tennis ball, for they call them Tennis-ball Trees. This fruit develops on a distinct stem at the junction of branch and branchlets. The leaves are dark, sickle-shaped, and covered with a waxy substance.

Agathis species are slow-growing, and have not been much developed for timber use by modern foresters, although in earlier days they were valued by the native populations. They still give one of our finest timbers, relatively knot-free due to the trees' habit of shedding lower branches as they grow.

All parts of the Kauri are rich in a particularly long-lasting resin used in the production of linoleum-type floor coverings and varnish. This resin often outlasts the trees themselves and becomes fossilized. It is known as copal, and there is a small industry in New Zealand, reclaiming it from fossil beds for commercial use.

Some fifteen Kauri species are listed, originating from Australia, New Zealand, Malaysia, the Philippines, Fiji, Tonga and New Caledonia, but nowadays many botanists seem to think that they may only be adaptations (though distinctly varied) of a single, original species.

The most common species are:

A. australis, the New Zealand Kauri, with cones 7.5cm in diameter.

A. moorei, the New Caledonian Kauri, with cones 12.5cm in length.

A. robusta, the Queensland Kauri. Cones 12cm in length and width.

A. vitiensis, the Fiji Tennis-ball Tree. Fast growing and the tallest species.

Kauris are propagated from seed.

Agathis australis
Kauri Pine

Agathis vitiensis
Tennis-ball Tree

ALEURITES

Candlenut
* **Evergreen /fast**
* **Oil-rich nuts**
  all year
* **Ht: to 20m /60ft** [T] [H]

Named from the Greek *aleuron* meaning floury, the striking Candlenut tree **A. moluccana** is found in hillside forests of the Pacific Islands and South-East Asia, where its pale, mealy foliage stands out from darker tropical vegetation. It is one of the great domesticated trees of the world, with a thousand uses, and has been adopted as the official tree emblem of Hawaii, where it was probably imported by the Polynesian ancestors.

The Kukui (as Hawaiians called it) used to be as important as the Coconut Palm. The timber had many uses, particularly for canoe building. A gum extracted from it strengthened the tapa cloth they made, which was also dyed with a pigment from the roots and seed shells.

The seed shells themselves were used as beads, and their kernels, rich in oil, were threaded on coconut leaf-ribs and burnt as candles — hence the common name Candlenut Tree.

The Candlenut may reach 20m in height and is densely clothed with hand-sized three- or five-lobed leaves, pale green, with a rusty fuzz on the undersides. The tiny white flowers, borne in panicles several times a year, are followed by clusters of 5cm nuts, which resemble a European walnut. A decorative variety, **A. moluccana remui,** is valued for its deep-lobed leaves.

Several closely related but smaller species are grown in South-East Asia, principally for their commercial value. They include the Japan Wood-oil Tree, **A. cordata,** which may reach 13m, has 3-5 lobed leaves and bears warty 2.5cm fruit with oil-rich seeds. The Tung-oil tree, **A. fordii,** which also grows to 13m, bears 3-lobed leaves and smooth, 7.5cm fruit. The tung oil extracted from these is used as a drying medium in paints and varnishes. The Mu-oil tree, **A. montana,** grows smaller still, to 8m only. Its leaves are 3-5 lobed, and the 4cm, smooth fruit produces an inferior quality oil.

All may be grown from seed or cuttings under heat, and are found in gardens throughout the world.

Aleurites moluccana
Candlenut Tree

Aleurites moluccana
Kukui, fruit

Alnus glutinosa
Common Alder

Alnus oregana
Red Alder

ALNUS

Alder
* **Deciduous /fast** C
* **Persistent catkins** T
* **Ht: 8-35m /24-120ft**

Closely related to the slim and graceful Birches (see **Betula**), the Northern Hemisphere's ubiquitous Alders are, like the Birches, water babies. You see them in places where the soil is deep and wet — by riversides, along the line of underground watercourses, around the rim of marshes or in low-lying hollows. Their massive roots help protect river banks from erosion. Their timber is so water-resistant that piles cut from it have supported the city of Venice for centuries. **Alnus** was the original Roman name for the tree.

Alders are in fact so common in Europe, Asia and the Americas that their value as a garden tree has been greatly underestimated. Quite apart from their wet-soil uses mentioned above, they are remarkably attractive trees, with a light, lacy appearance in winter when they are bare, and a pleasant covering of glossy long-stemmed leaves that flutter in spring and summer breezes.

The trees have a slim, upright shape with generally horizontal or slightly weeping branches that are festooned for much of the year with their curious flowers. The flowers are of two sorts: the female, borne in long dangling catkins; and the male, which are formed as small woody cones, rather like a conifer's.

Many species of **Alnus** make good street trees as well as garden specimens, and all of them are easily propagated from seed. The exceptions, as usual, are the fancy-leafed cultivars, which must be grafted.

Alders will resist a reasonable degree of frost and are quite happy in climates with up to subtropical temperatures, particularly the American west coast species. These include: **A. jorullensis,** a partly evergreen species from Mexico which grows to 8m; **A. oregana,** the Red Alder, a big tree to 23m, widely planted in Los Angeles; **A. rhombifolia,** the White Alder, which may reach 35m. The European species are **A. cordata,** the Italian Alder, and **A. glutinosa,** the Common Alder, both growing to 25m.

ANNONA

Custard Apple,
Cherimoya, Soursop
* **Evergreen/
medium fast**
* **Summer fruits**
* **Ht: 7-10m/20-30ft**

T H

The **Annonas** or Custard Apples include about fifty species of small trees and shrubs from the tropics of Asia, Africa and the Americas. All of them are grown world-wide in warm climates for their delicious and re-freshing fruits, which are borne heavily. The name *annona* is Latin, and means 'yearly produce'.

Annonas grow readily from seed, or bud grafts; few of the useful species will pass 8m in height, and about half that in width. The alternate leaves are noticeably glossy and pleasantly scented, the flowers quite unin-teresting. They would probably not be grown if it were not for the splendid fruit harvest, though many would say that these are an acquired taste.

Species commonly seen in fruit shops are the richly flavoured Custard Apple or Cherimoya, **A. cherimolia;** the refreshing and acid Soursop, **A. muricata;** the Bullock's Heart, **A. reticulata;** and the Sugar Apple, **A. squamosa.**

Curiously, in spite of their human appetite appeal, both fruits and leaves of all species have insecticidal properties.

Annona muricata
Soursop

Annona squamosa
Sugar Apple

Annona cherimolia
Custard Apple

Araucaria araucana
Monkey Puzzle Tree

Araucaria bidwillii
Bunya Bunya

ARAUCARIA

Bunya Bunya,
Monkey Puzzle,
Norfolk Island Pine
* **Evergreen/fast**
* **Very large cones**
* **Ht: 35-70m/100-200ft**

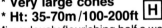

Miraculously flourishing half a world apart on both fringes of the vast South Pacific, the grand and glorious **Araucarias** are outstanding conifers, all the more remarkable for being found only in the Southern Hemisphere, where conifers are rare.

Named for the Araucanian natives of South America, the true Monkey Puzzle Tree, **Araucaria araucana,** was the first of these to be introduced to cultivation in 1795. A stiff and starchy construction of angular, scaled branches, it is popular in cooler climates and quite hardy in the British Isles, for which its four cousins are much too tender.

The first of these, the Bunya Bunya, **A. bidwillii,** would seem like an artist's fantasy if it did not already exist. The squat trunk, rather like a fat elephant's foot, tapers rapidly and is surrounded by stiff branches nearly as long as itself. At the top of mature trees, these open out like umbrella spokes into a great bird's nest affair. All branches develop into scaly branchlets rather like Medusa's snake-hair. The scales themselves are razor sharp. The great fruits, which develop high up, have the size and shape of a giant pineapple, and contain scarlet seeds which were a great delicacy to the Australian Aborigines.

The other species are:

A. columellaris, the slender Cook Pine, found only in New Caledonia and nearby islets. This grows to 70m in height, and has an exaggeratedly columnar shape, losing its lower branches, which are replaced by fuzzy twigs.

A. cunninghamii, the Hoop Pine, is from eastern Australia, and looks rather like an architect's model of a tree — all green sponge rubber and fuzz. It also grows to 70m, has needle-like juvenile leaves, with mature foliage in dense tufts at the end of bare branches. It is an important timber tree.

Finally, there is the most outstanding of all, **A. heterophylla,** the Norfolk Island Pine, which grows densely on that island, but is also native to coastal areas of north-east Au-

ARAUCARIA (continued)

stralia. This tree is sometimes called the Star Pine from the regular star shapes formed by its horizontal layers of branchlets.

A. heterophylla is normally a completely salt-resistant tree, all parts being protected by a waxy coating. It was much used in earlier days for formal planting along beachfront esplanades, but in recent years, these beachfront trees have been dying in parts of eastern Australia.

Dendrologists cannot be certain, but they believe this is due to the pollution of coastal waters by synthetic detergents. Sea breezes spray the trees with these detergents which eat away the protective wax, leaving the tree open to salt burn. It is the trees near the big cities that are the worst affected, but they were also planted first, and it may yet prove to be just the onset of old age.

Araucarias are not cut much for timber, but are of great value in preventing seaside erosion. The leaves are modified into overlapping scales.

Araucaria heterophylla
Norfolk Island Pine ▶

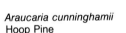

Araucaria cunninghamii
Hoop Pine

Araucaria bidwillii
fruit

25

ARTOCARPUS

Breadfruit, Uru
* **Evergreen /fast**
* **Summer fruit**
* **Ht: to 17m /50ft**

It was the Breadfruit, as every schoolboy knows, that caused Captain Bligh's undoing on the *Bounty*. These unappetizing fruit species come from South-East Asia and only one, **A. altilis,** was carried into the Pacific during Polynesian migrations.

They are large, tropical relatives of the humble mulberry, which they even resemble on a vast scale.

The peeled fruit can be baked, boiled or pickled when unripe, and will keep for years if buried in a pit. Ripened, it becomes sweet and tangy and can be pounded into a paste for dessert. The deeply lobed leaves (possibly the most beautiful of any tree) may be 1m in length, and were used for roofing, clothing and wrapping foods for the oven. The Hawaiians call it **ulu,** the Tahitians **uru.**

Artocarpus is propagated from shoots which arise spontaneously from the roots. It must have a hot, humid climate and fruits most heavily in the summer wet season.

Artocarpus altilis
Breadfruit

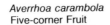

Averrhoa carambola
Five-corner Fruit

AVERRHOA

Five-corner Fruit,
Carambole
* **Evergreen /fast**
* **Late summer fruits**
* **Ht: to 10m /30ft**

Yet another warm-climate tree genus with edible fruit, **Averrhoas** make handsome specimen trees for the semi-tropical garden.

A. carambola, the Carambole, Five-corner Fruit or Star Fruit, is a light tree, reaching 10m. Its leaves have five to eleven leaflets and the flowers appear from branches, trunk and twigs. The fruits are sharply five-cornered and look as if carved from orange wax. Inside is a mass of sweet watery pulp, tasting like a cross between apricots and passionfruit. Delicious!

They are grown commercially in California, northern Australia and parts of Africa.

26

BARRINGTONIA

Hotu,
Fish Poison Tree
 * **Evergreen/slow**
 * **Red new foliage**
 * **Ht: to 5m/15ft**   T H

Scattered about seaside areas of the Indian
and Pacific Oceans is a broad, handsome
tree that has every appearance of the American Magnolia **(M. grandiflora).** It has the
same buttressed trunk and leathery, glossy
leaves. But there the resemblance stops, for
the plump flower buds at branches' end open
into brilliant pink and white puffballs of fragrant stamens up to 15cm in diameter. How
often have I tried to photograph one on the
tree itself, but alas, they never appear till late
evening, and drop before dawn, scattering
the lawns or beach around with their fading
beauty.

The tree (named for an eighteenth century
naturalist called Daines Barrington) is **Barringtonia asiatica,** and the most remarkable
thing about it is the heart-shaped, four-sided
fruits that develop after the flowers. These
consist of a corky, fibrous husk containing
one seed. They are completely buoyant, and
will float for long distances, thus accounting
for the tree's widespread location in
beachside areas.

Native fishermen all over the Pacific use
them as floats for their nets, and even more
importantly, they have discovered that the
grated seed, sprinkled into a lagoon, will stun
fish and bring them quickly to the surface
where they can be picked up by hand. Because of the seed pod's shape, the Tahitians
call the tree *hotu,* meaning the human heart,
from which legend tells them it sprang.

One of the Hotu's most attractive features
is the irregular colouring and fall of the
leaves, which assume brilliant autumn tones
at any time of the year.

Although generally found by the shore,
Barringtonia grows equally well inland, and
makes a fine garden specimen in warm climates, as do the closely related **B. acutan-
gula** and **B. racemosa.** Both of these are
taller trees, reaching 15m. The former bears
spectacular clusters of bright red blossom;
the latter, white.

Barringtonias are propagated from seed,
and need a subtropical climate.

Barringtonia asiatica
Fish Poison Tree

Barringtonia asiatica
young foliage

27

BETULA

Birch
* **Deciduous /fast**
* **Autumn colour**
* **Ht: 20-35m /60-100ft**

C
T

Hardiest of the deciduous broad-leafed trees, the slim and beautiful birches, 'Ladies of the Woods' as the poet Coleridge christened them, include over thirty-five species from all three continents of the Northern Hemisphere. Vast forests of them spread in a band across Scandinavia, the USSR and North America, thinning out and gradually shrinking into shrubby growth as their range blurs into the Arctic tundra.

In their southern limits, they tend to huddle decoratively in small groups on poor sandy soil or gravel beds along rivers, but in horticultural use they grow well in any soil as long as the drainage is good.

As a rule, birches are among the lightest of trees, tall and slender, with vividly coloured bark that tends to peel away in horizontal strips. In the species most commonly grown in cooler-climate gardens (they are no use at all in subtropical climates), the bark is silvergrey or white; but there are others with reddish-brown, black and yellow bark. The leaves usually are slightly more angular than oval, deeply toothed and in most species lightly borne and fluttering in the least sign of a breeze. Insignificant flowers are followed by catkins made up of a series of winged seeds. These catkins generally hang and disintegrate when ripe.

Birches (**Betula** to give them their original Roman name) grow readily from seed except for a few fancy-leafed varieties which must be grafted. The incredibly fine branches of most species weep gracefully, and at one time were tied together as brooms, and to tan schoolboys' backsides. The deciduous leaves turn to purest gold before they fall in late autumn.

The Swedish Birch (**B. pendula** CV 'Dalecarlica') is particularly worth seeking out

Betula CV 'Dalecarlica'
Swedish Birch

BETULA (continued)

for its deeply-cut leaves, while **B. pendula** CV 'Youngii' or Young's Weeping Birch is the perfect specimen tree for a poolside position. Its branches, which weep in an exaggerated fashion, will need support, however, for the tree is relatively shallow-rooted and may topple.

Birch timber is used for modern Scandinavian furniture and kitchen utensils, and is also laminated into some of the world's finest plywood. The bark of all species is remarkably tough and water-resistant and was long used by North American Indians for their canoes.

The European Birch grows to 20m, its cultivars slightly smaller. The American Canoe Birch and Black Birch to 35m.

Betula papyrifera
Canoe Birch

Betula pendula
European White Birch

Betula lenta
Cherry Birch

BISCHOFIA

Toog Tree, Koka
* **Deciduous/fast**
* **Decorative berries** H
* **Ht: to 23m/70ft**

One of the most important timber trees of Indonesia and South-East Asia, the Toog or Koka Tree **(Bischofia javanica)** is found in a wide tropical band well out into Polynesia. It is a popular and decorative specimen tree in warm climate gardens, growing straight and smooth to 23m.

The Toog is semi-deciduous, with bronze-green compound leaves divided into three pointed, long-oval leaflets which turn bright red and fall from time to time. The bark is smooth and grey, and the female flowers develop into clusters of tiny pea-sized fruits which may be reddish-brown, yellow or almost black.

The timber, while not of the finest quality, has many uses in less sophisticated communities.

Bischofia javanica
Toog Tree

Blighia sapida
Akee Apple

BLIGHIA

Akee Apple
* **Evergreen/fast** T
* **Summer fruit**
* **Ht: to 13m/40ft** H

Captain Bligh may have lost his reputation over the breadfruit trees, but his name is remembered by another attractive fruiting tree, **Blighia sapida,** the Akee Apple.

Originally from West Africa, it is seen in tropical gardens everywhere, the only one of its genus. Growing to 13m in height, it is a handsome ornamental tree with shining compound leaves consisting of up to ten oblong leaflets of graduated sizes, the largest towards the tip.

The five-petalled flowers are fragrant and greenish; the fruit, a rather pear-shaped, ribbed capsule, varies from a pale apricot to ruby pink in colour. The flesh is said to be poisonous when green, but is delicious and nutritious when ripe.

Blighia will grow in any moist, rich soil. It is propagated from seed and will stand several degrees of frost.

BOMBAX

Silk Cotton Tree, Barrigon,
Shaving Brush Tree
* **Deciduous /fast** [T]
* **Dense foliage**
* **Ht: 15-35m /45-100ft** [H]

From tropical forests of Asia, South America and Africa comes a genus of splendid specimen trees called **Bombax.** Their rather jingoistic name is in fact an ancient Greek word for cotton, although the filaments obtained from their bulky seedpods are far too fine to spin, and are used instead as a substitute for kapok.

B. malabaricum, the Red Silk Cotton Tree from South-East Asia, is the most commonly seen species, in gardens of northern Australia, Hong Kong, Africa, Hawaii and many other places. It is a tall tree, reaching 35m and more, with a widely buttressed trunk at maturity. Easily raised from seed, this **Bombax** needs deep soil and lots of moisture all year round to grow really well and produce its stunning crop of 17.5cm red flowers in early spring. These appear at the ends of branches shortly after the tree loses its foliage for a brief period in winter.

The leaves of **B. malabaricum** are strikingly digitate and up to 50cm across, consisting of three to seven widely spread leaflets. The trunk is sometimes spiny, and the tree may need a little pruning and staking when young.

Closely related **B. ellipticum** is from Mexico, and also deciduous. Its compound leaves, of five leaflets only, may be 45cm in diameter, and are a handsome coppery-red when young. It is a stark, heavy-branched tree with bark patterned in a magnificent snakeskin effect of grey and green. The flowers consist almost entirely of a mass of white or pink stamens, resembling a shaving brush, and are followed by 10cm capsules full of greenish fibre which is used as kapok substitute.

B. barrigon is an even smaller ornamental tree from tropical America, rarely reaching 15m in height. Its 30cm compound leaves have seven to nine leaflets. The white flowers develop into 17.5cm pods. It is easily recognized by its heavy, buttressed trunk.

Bombax malabaricum
Red Silk Cotton

Bombax ellipticum
bark detail

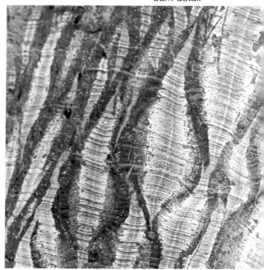

31

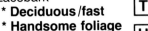

BRACHYCHITON

Kurrajong, Bottle Tree, Lacebark

* **Deciduous/fast**　T
* **Handsome foliage**
* **Ht: 10-35m/30-100ft**　H

Considered by many to be Australia's most spectacular genus of flowering trees, the Kurrajongs (**Brachychiton** spp.) are maddeningly irregular in their flowering habits. But throughout the warm weather, they are decorative and valuable shade trees.

Brachychitons are the most variable of trees — variable in size, shape of trunk and leaves, and size and colouring of flowers, which are generally bell-shaped. Those which are native to the semi-tropical forests of Australia's moist east coast tend to grow tall and flower profusely on the bare tree after leaf fall, in late spring. These include: **B. acerifolium,** the Illawarra Flame, with large Maple-like leaves; **B. bidwillii,** the Pink Lacebark, with furry, heart-shaped foliage; and **B. discolor,** the White Lacebark, with three to seven lobed leaves, shiny above, furry on the reverse. This develops a heavily buttressed trunk and often branches at a great height. Other Kurrajongs, native to the dry Australian outback, are generally smaller in size with bloated water-storing trunks, like the illustrated **B. rupestre,** known as the Queensland Bottle Tree. The new summer foliage is often used for fodder in drought-stricken areas.

A peculiarity of the Kurrajongs is the extreme leaf variation. On one tree of **B. populneum,** for instance, you may find simple pointed leaves, rather like a poplar's, and others that are long and angular, divided into anything from three to nine pointed lobes. Because of this, the tree is sometimes listed as **B. diversifolia,** though there is no true species of this name.

All the Kurrajongs thrive in warm, dryish climates such as California, South Africa and the Mediterranean, but the desert species do not do well in the moister subtropics like Hawaii and Hong Kong.

Most Kurrajong species are cultivated for their decorative and shade-giving qualities. There are many intermediate hybrids, and all can be grown from seed or cuttings.

Brachychiton populneum
Kurrajong

Brachychiton rupestre
Queensland Bottle Tree

CALLITRIS

Cypress Pine
 * **Evergreen**/fast   C
 * **Conifer**
 * Ht: 7-35m/20-100ft   T

The most commonly seen conifers in the Australian landscape, the native **Callitris** or Cypress Pines are found in all states of Australia, and have been widely grown in other countries because of their resistance to dry, sandy conditions. They will survive where no self-respecting pine or spruce would think of taking a foothold, and are typically found dotting the western plains beyond Australia's coastal Great Dividing Range.

The trees are generally of tall cypress shape with extremely fine cypress-like foliage, the leaves adapted into the tiniest of scales. The bark is usually dark, the cones small and divided into six segments of variable length.

Apart from their drought-resistant qualities, the Cypress Pines are greatly valued for their pale, colourfully knot-marked timber, which is completely resistant to termites. This wood is hard and dense and takes a beautiful polish. It is often used for flooring or feature panelling.

Commonly cultivated species are the 26m White Cypress Pine, or Murray Pine, **C. columellaris,** with brilliant green scale-leaves and dark brown 1cm cones split into six irregular segments. An upright, columnar tree, it resembles the Italian Cypress at a distance.

C. cupressiformis, the true Cypress Pine, has a bluish cast to its foliage, produces three-celled cones. It is more pyramidal in shape, rarely passing 7m in height.

The Rottnest Island Pine, **C. preissii** is from South and West Australia, and the giant of the family, reaching 35m in the wild. Its leaf-scales are more rounded, the flattened cones up to 3.5cm in diameter. They may be borne singly or in clusters.

Finally, there is the Oyster Bay Pine, **C. rhomboidea,** which may reach 13m and is common around Sydney. The sparse leaf-scales are small and bluish, the cones spherical, divided in three sections.

All **Callitris** may be propagated from seed or cuttings struck with bottom heat.

Callitris columellaris
White Cypress Pine

Callitris cupressiformis
fruit detail

Caprica papaya
Paw Paw, Papaya

Carica papaya
fruit detail

CARICA

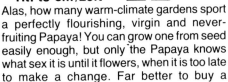

Papaya, Paw Paw
  * **Evergreen /fast**
  * **Summer fruit**
  * **Ht: to 8m /25ft**   T H

Alas, how many warm-climate gardens sport a perfectly flourishing, virgin and never-fruiting Papaya! You can grow one from seed easily enough, but only the Papaya knows what sex it is until it flowers, when it is too late to make a change. Far better to buy a guaranteed bisexual plant from a reputable nursery.

The Papaya or **Carica papaya** is hardly a tree at all by most criteria. It has a succulent, hollow trunk which never develops into hard wood. It scarcely branches unless damaged, just grows continually taller to 8m, dropping its old foliage as it goes, and is always topped with a palm-like crown of magnificent compound leaves.

34

Male Papayas or Paw Paws bear their creamy-green flowers in dangling racemes, the females as small, neat clusters. Only female trees will fruit, of course, producing masses of melon-sized fruit close to the trunk among the leaves. These have a thick, delicious pulp and are hollow.

Papayas will stand occasional frost, though both leaves and trunks may be badly marked.

CARPINUS

Hornbeam, Ironwood
* **Deciduous/slow** [C]
* **Autumn colour**
* **Ht: to 12m/40ft** [T]

All natives of the Northern Hemisphere, the thirty-odd species of Hornbeam, considered small shade trees by cool-climate standards, grow 7-17m in height. The most commonly planted, European **Carpinus betulus,** may reach 21m in a forest, but rarely half that in cultivation. Used in many lands for street planting, it has a pyramidal form when young, gradually spreading wide as it is high, with weeping outer branches. The distinctive ovate-oblong leaves are sharply toothed and noticeably veined. Borne alternately, they remain on the tree until well into autumn, turning gold in a cool-temperate climate, dark red in a particularly cold year. Hardy trees, they resist winter cold, and prefer generally moist soils; not recommended for dry-winter or desert areas.

The timber is strong and dense, used often for the manufacture of small articles such as tool handles.

Small flowers hang in 12.5cm catkins, later develop into a drooping chain of small nuts, each enclosed in a 3-lobed, leafy bract. These clusters look quite decorative hanging among the foliage, spinning and turning in the lightest breeze.

Hornbeams are grown easily from autumn-sown seed, though the many cultivars must be propagated by grafting. They include 'Columnaris' with a slender vertical habit; 'Pendula' with drooping branches; 'Purpurea' with purplish young foliage. In parts of Europe and the Middle East, Hornbeams are sometimes close-planted

Carpinus betulus
Hornbeam

Carpinus betulus
fruit detail

into a particularly dense hedge. American species **C. caroliniana** and Asian **C. japonica** and **C. laxiflora** are also grown locally. They have shorter catkins.

Carya laciniata
Shellbark Hickory

CARYA

Hickory, Pecan
* **Deciduous/fast**
* **Summer nuts /**
  autumn colour
* **Ht: 13-55m/40-150ft**

C
T

All Hickories in cultivation are North American in origin, though there are one or two Asiatic species. The shame is that so few of them *are* in cultivation outside their native area. They grow fast, straight and tall, bear delicious nuts (Pecans ripen on one species) and turn an unbelievable pure gold in autumn. They are, however, very difficult to transplant, particularly when they reach any size.

So the only solution is to do what the squirrels do and bury the nuts. They come up in no time, but many years will pass before you can pick your own crop. Still, if you can put the idea of pecan pie and pralines out of your mind and just think of the tree for its own beautiful sake, you will try to locate one among your nursery acquaintances.

Carya species like a deep, rich soil, and enjoy a surprisingly wide climatic range, from Canada's Quebec province right down to Mexico in their native North America.

The Hickories are closely related to the walnuts (see **Juglans),** and like them, bear handsome, fragrant compound leaves, each consisting of a number of spear-shaped leaflets (ranging five to seventeen according to the species). Flowers of both sexes appear on the one tree, the male in long triple catkins, the female in small spikes at ends of branches. The nuts vary in both shape and colour according to species.

C. illinoinensis, the Pecan, bears the best nuts. The Shagbark Hickory, **C. ovata,** is the most striking tree, growing twice as tall as it does wide. The trunk of a mature specimen is decorated with patches of tattered bark. The Shagbarks make a fine spectacle with brilliant autumn colour.

The Pignut or Small-fruited Hickory, **C. glabra,** is the most manageable size for the home garden, rarely passing 13m. It is slower in growth, round-headed rather than columnar.

The scientific name **Carya** is from *karya,* the old Greek word for their close relatives, the Walnuts.

Carya illinoinensis
Pecan nuts

CASTANEA

Chestnut, Chinquapin
* **Deciduous/fast**
* **Summer nuts,**
   autumn colour
* **Ht: 10-30m/30-90ft**

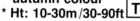

Never a large genus at the best of times (there are fewer than a dozen species found in all three continents of the Northern Hemisphere), the tall-growing deciduous Chestnuts appear to be doomed by an Asiatic fungus that destroys the tree's circulation. They have been virtually wiped out right across the North American continent, and it seems only a matter of time before the same fungus appears in Europe.

But they are still a good specimen choice in parts of the world to which they are not native, particularly in the Southern Hemisphere.

The most loved species is the Spanish or Sweet Chestnut, **Castanea sativa,** from Europe, Asia Minor and North Africa. These are grown principally for the nutritious brown nuts which ripen enclosed in a prickly burr-like casing in late summer. They are often roasted as a winter delicacy, or pureed with vanilla and sugar as a delicious dessert.

Castanea sativa
fruit detail

Castanea sativa
Spanish Chestnut

Spanish Chestnuts propagate easily from seed, grow rapidly in deep, acid soil, sometimes bearing fruit in the third year, and are undamaged by hot dry summers.

The profuse foliage consists of single 22.5cm leaves, long and pointed, sharply toothed and with downy reverses. The flowers appear in long drooping golden catkins in early summer, and the burr-encased nuts (at first green, later brown) appear late in the season and remain on the tree after leaf fall.

Mature Chestnut trees (no longer common, alas!) bear their bark in a distinctive spiral pattern and may reach 13m in trunk circumference. They have been known to live several thousand years.

North American Chestnut species **C. dentata** and **C. pumila** are known as Chinquapin, from their Indian name, but are now virtually extinct.

Asiatic species **C. crenata** and **C. mollissima** are much smaller trees, raised more for timber than for nuts.

All Chestnuts sucker strongly from around the trunk.

Casuarina littoralis
Black Sheoke

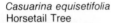

Casuarina equisetifolia
Horsetail Tree

CASUARINA

Sheoke, Ironwood
* **Evergreen /fast**
* **Weeping branchlets**
* **Ht: 15-25m /45-75ft**

T
H

'Out of place in the wanton tropics' was how author Somerset Maugham described the **Casuarina** trees. And as usual, his description was apt; they are the sort of ghostly, leafless plants you expect to find in dry, desert areas. Yet there they are on the coasts and watercourses of many lands and islands, from East Africa, through southern India and Australia right out to far Tahiti and the South Pacific islands.

Their handsome, figured timber is as hard as the Oak which has been charmingly mis-spelled in their popular name; the soft needle-like foliage never ceases to move in the trade winds that murmur through the weeping branchlets making a continuous 'sshh' sound which some poetic soul has incorporated into their name. More practical botanists chose the name **Casuarina** because the foliage resembles the feathers of Australia's cassowary bird.

The **Casuarinas** are indeed strange and mysterious trees, closely related to no other, and possessed of many powers, both real and imaginary. In coastal and riverside situations their massive root systems are great sand-binders, although they take so much nourishment out of the soil that nothing can grow nearby.

The fine foliage, which consists of branchlets, not leaves, makes an excellent windbreak and gives soft, luminous shade. In older days, the iron-hard timber was used for war clubs, boomerangs and other weapons, and also for carpenters' tools.

The **Casuarinas** have always had magical associations, the Tahitians believing they sprang from the bodies of dead warriors whose hair became foliage, and whose blood flowed again as the red sap.

Casuarinas do have leaves, but they are so small it is difficult to see them with the naked eye. They have developed into tiny scales which clothe the weeping branchlets. From the base of these scales appear the tiny flowers which cause the branchlets to turn red and fuzzy in late spring.

CEDRELA

Toon, Cigar Box Tree [T]
* **Deciduous /fast**
* **Spring leaf colour** [H]
* **Ht: 15-35m /40-100ft**

The delightful, small genus **Cedrela** (fewer than twenty species world-wide) from South-East Asia, the Caribbean and tropical America, is named after the giant Cedars of Lebanon, North Africa and India. **Cedrela** is the diminutive form of the Greek **kedros** meaning a Cedar, although it is not even remotely related. Whereas Cedars are enormous, cool-climate conifers and evergreen, the **Cedrelas** are mostly subtropical and deciduous.

Then how did they get their name? From the heartwood's strong resemblance to Cedar wood, in both colour and grain, and also in the aromatic fragrance which makes the timber completely insect repellent.

The **Cedrelas** more strongly resemble **Ailanthus,** to which they are related, but they have a slighter appearance and often have heavily buttressed roots. The leaves are long and pinnate with many leaflets and are generally deciduous. In the case of the Chinese Cedar or Toon **(C. sinensis)** the young foliage is a delicate pink, onion-flavoured and quite edible. It also turns a magnificent gold in autumn, when the tree's splendid shape is fully revealed.

C. sinensis is one of the world's most desirable timber trees. In horticultural practice, the tree is grown for its decorative spring foliage. The tiny flowers are in weeping panicles and followed by small fruits from which the trees are propagated.

C. sinensis is a cooler climate tree, while the South American Cigar Box Cedar **(C. odorata)** is fully tropical in its needs. A much larger tree (to 35m) it is occasionally grown as an ornamental, but is more highly valued as a timber tree, its fragrant, insect repellent wood being used for cigar boxes, and also to line storage cupboards.

Leaves are smaller than in the Chinese species, but its seed capsules much larger.

The Australian Red Cedar was long named **C. toona,** but is now classified as **Toona australis** (see **Toona**).

Cedrela sinensis
Chinese Toon

Cedrela odorata
Cigar Box Cedar

CEDRUS

Cedar, Deodar ⌈C⌉
* **Evergreen/slow** ⌈T⌉
* **Summer cones**
* **Ht: 35-70m/100-200ft**

The Cedars are one of the few genera to be known by the same name for thousands of years. To the Romans they were already **Cedrus;** to the Greeks before them *kedros;* and to the writers of the Old Testament a name very similar. They were regarded as the most precious of all timbers, a gift from God himself. The great stones of the pyramids were rolled into place on mighty Cedar trunks, and later the Crusaders felled them for the construction of their palaces in the Holy Land.

As a result, the magnificent Cedars of Lebanon are today very rare in their native land, and even the survivors not as old as is often claimed.

There are four species generally recognized: the Deodar or Indian Cedar **(C. deodar),** the Atlantic Cedar **(C. atlantica),** the Cedar of Lebanon **(C. libani)** and the Cyprus Cedar, all with many varieties of leaf colour and habit. Many botanists believe they are all regional remnants of a single tree species that once flourished widely from Africa across to India. But they have developed minor differences in their present native habitats. The Deodar of the Himalayas is by far the largest, reaching up to 70m — a giant of a tree with a trunk girth to 12m and a distinct weeping habit, particularly in young specimens. The Atlantic or Mt Atlas Cedar from the mountains of Morocco is next, with a pyramidal habit and faster growth. Its form **C.a. glauca pendula,** a favourite tree for parks, has blue-grey leaves and branches dragging on the ground.

The biblical Cedar of Lebanon is a majestic giant of a tree, flat-topped and often wider than its height; while the Cyprus Cedar is a relative pygmy, dwarfed by the poor soil of its native island.

All Cedars demand a deep, rich soil for maximum growth, and particularly a porous subsoil. They are really too large for the average home, but make splendid specimens in large mountain gardens.

Cedrus atlantica aurea
Golden Atlantic Cedar

Cedrus atlantica
cone detail

CEIBA

Kapok Tree
 * **Deciduous /fast**
 * **Summer pods**
 * **Ht: to 50m /150ft**   H

Found in the tropic zones of both the old and the new world is a small genus of gigantic deciduous trees, once of great commercial value. They are the strange-looking **Ceiba** or Kapok trees, whose large, hanging seed pods are filled with the fine, downy fibre now largely superseded by synthetics as a stuffing for pillows and quilts. They have tall, straight, often spiny trunks that may reach 50m in height and up to 3m in diameter.

Branches of **C. pentandra** (*ceiba* is its original native name) are sparse, and generally arranged in irregular whorls around the trunk. The leaves are pinnate, with five to seven spear-shaped leaflets around 15cm long.

Whitish spring flowers are followed by elliptical capsules that contain kapok and may be up to 25cm long. Kapok trees were imported commercially to South-East Asia and old trees are often found there.

The **Ceibas** are strictly tropical, with about ten species in cultivation.

Ceiba pentandra
Kapok Tree ▶

Ceiba pentandra
Kapok pod

Celtis occidentalis
Sugarberry

CELTIS

Nettle Tree, Hackberry
* **Deciduous /fast**
* **Autumn colour /**
  berries
* **Ht: 20-40m /60-120ft**

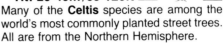 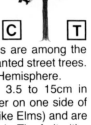

Many of the **Celtis** species are among the world's most commonly planted street trees. All are from the Northern Hemisphere.

Individual leaves (from 3.5 to 15cm in length) are frequently larger on one side of their stem than the other (like Elms) and are extremely rough to the touch. The fruits (the size and colour of an edible green pea) are sometimes eaten in countries where food is scarce.

All **Celtis** species may be propagated from cuttings or seeds. They are useful, fast-growing shade trees and come into their own in autumn. In cooler climates, the serrated leaves change to a pale yellow, and the fruits may become orange, red, purple and almost black. **Celtis** are reasonably frost-hardy.

Ceratonia siliqua
Carob Bean

CERATONIA

Carob Tree,
St John's Bread
* **Evergreen /slow**
* **Summer pods**
* **Ht: to 15m /45ft**

If you've ever visualized John the Baptist munching on grasshoppers, then think again! The locusts which sustained the good saint were fruits of the Carob or Locust tree, **Ceratonia siliqua,** a native of the Mediterranean.

It is a useful tree for dry and perennially drought-stricken areas, where its heavy foliage provides valuable shade, and the great crop of 15cm pods make a useful stock fodder. They are said to be very rich in both sugar and protein, and are used to make a chocolate substitute.

The **Ceratonia** is evergreen, ultimately reaching a height of 15m, though obviously a slow grower in arid areas. Its pinnate leaves are up to 25cm long; the flowers red and hardly noticeable. The pods follow in summer, but only on female trees. **Ceratonia** is easily grown from seed.

CERCIDIPHYLLUM

Katsura Tree
* **Deciduous/slow**
* **Autumn colour**
* **Ht: to 12m/40ft**

A beautiful deciduous tree from Japan, **Cercidiphyllum japonicum** is rarely seen elsewhere, except as a park specimen. It enjoys a cool, moist climate with protection from drying sun and winds, bears handsome, heart-shaped 10cm blue-green leaves with red stems, and often reddish veins. The foliage colours beautifully in autumn, and the effect is most stunning after a dry summer.

Cercidiphyllum commonly develops multiple trunks from the base, giving it the effect of a small grove of slender saplings. At all times, it has a light airy appearance, and though it rarely passes 12m in cultivation, can be much larger in the wild. Give it plenty of moisture in the summer, propagate from spring seed.

Cercidiphyllum japonicum
Katsura Tree

Chamaecyparis nootkaensis
Nootka Cypress

CHAMAECYPARIS

False Cypress,
Lawson Cypress
* **Evergreen/fast**
* **Colourful foliage**
* **Ht: 30-40m/90-120ft**

The False Cypresses, **Chamaecyparis,** form one of the smallest genera in botany — no more than about eight species. But due to their inherent instability, in both habit and coloration, the cultivated varieties developed from those eight species would fill a book. They must surely be the most popular, the most widely planted evergreens in horticultural practice.

At one time they were included by botanists among the true Cypresses (see **Cupressus**), but were placed in a separate genus of their own earlier this century; the criteria for separation included the number of seeds produced per scale, and the formation of the first juvenile leaves.

Why the name **Chamaecyparis,** meaning dwarf cypress, was chosen is a complete mystery! None of the original species grows to less than 25m in the wild, and the popular Lawson Cypress **(C. lawsoniana)** prefers to

Chamaecyparis lawsoniana
Lawson Cypress, fruit

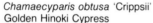

Chamaecyparis obtusa 'Crippsii'
Golden Hinoki Cypress

CHAMAECYPARIS (continued)

shoot up to about 70m in its moist coastal forests of northern California and southern Oregon.

The Nootka Cypress **(C. nootkaensis)** comes from the same general area, the White Cypress **(C. thyoides)** from eastern North America. The others are all from Japan, China and Taiwan.

Why are these variable trees so popular in cultivation? Well, they are easy to propagate, easy to move at any size, and never need pruning. Added to which, their dainty foliage comes in almost every imaginable shade of green, gold and grey-blue, allowing for considerable colour interest in the evergreen garden.

Habits vary from dwarf to upright.

CHRYSOPHYLLUM

Star Apple
 * **Evergreen /fast**   C
 * **Spring fruits**
 * **Ht: 10-17m /30-50ft**   T

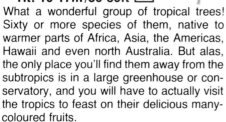

What a wonderful group of tropical trees! Sixty or more species of them, native to warmer parts of Africa, Asia, the Americas, Hawaii and even north Australia. But alas, the only place you'll find them away from the subtropics is in a large greenhouse or conservatory, and you will have to actually visit the tropics to feast on their delicious many-coloured fruits.

Chrysophyllum means golden or shining leaves, and that's precisely the effect you get standing beneath them, for their evergreen foliage is backed with silky hairs which have a strangely iridescent effect: gold, copper or even silver.

The Star Apple **(C. cainito)** from Central America and the West Indies is the most common species, now planted extensively right around the world. It is a tall tree, sometimes reaching 17m in height, and at a distance has a close resemblance to the European Copper Beech (see **Fagus**). The leaves are pointed, oblong and about 10cm in length, borne alternately on slim, often weeping branchlets.

The flowers are small and white, almost undetectable beneath the leaves, but they develop into shining apple-sized fruits, bright green at first, then ripening through a rosy flush to a vivid red-violet. They are quite delectable, full of cool, refreshing snow-white pulp with a puzzling flavour. Is it peach or persimmon? The popular name of Star Apple comes from the arrangement of the black seeds. Cut through a fruit, you'll see the seeds radiating in the form of a star.

The Star Apple's one requirement, apart from a hot climate, is year-round water.

A related species is the Jamaican Plum, **C. oliviforme,** which is altogether smaller, though also from the Caribbean. It grows to 10m, has 7.5cm red-backed leaves, and bears 2cm, tasty berries coloured a deep purple. Both species are propagated by seeds or ripened cuttings.

Chrysophyllum cainito
Star Apple

Chrysophyllum, fruit

45

Cinnamomum camphora
Camphor Laurel

CINNAMOMUM

Camphor Laurel,
Cinnamon
* **Evergreen /fast**
* **Pink spring foliage**
* **Ht: 10-35m /30-100ft**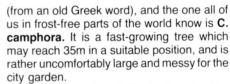

Marvellously fragrant in all its parts, the Asian Camphor Laurel is the most commonly grown and decorative of a large genus of aromatic trees. There are over 250 species found in the south of China, India, Malaysia and Australia, many of them highly valued in commerce as the source of a variety of gums and spices.

Cinnamomum is their botanical name

(from an old Greek word), and the one all of us in frost-free parts of the world know is **C. camphora.** It is a fast-growing tree which may reach 35m in a suitable position, and is rather uncomfortably large and messy for the city garden.

The trunk may reach 2m in diameter, the branches are heavy and can easily span 35m in a mature tree. The bark is grey and fissured, the leaves roundly pointed and a delightful apple-green in colour. The Camphor Laurel bears masses of tiny, fuzzy greenish yellow flowers in spring, followed by pea-sized black berries. But the best display is in early spring, when the entire tree performs a stunning striptease. First there is a flush of new pink foliage from top to toe, then almost

46

CINNAMOMUM (continued)

overnight, all the old leaves drop at once, making quite a litter.

Camphor Laurel leaves are not very good for compost, as they break down slowly, but they do make a delightful fragrant fire, for they are the source of medicinal camphor. The timber is also impregnated with it, so be sure to save dead branches for winter firewood. Camphorwood is light, pale and insect repellent. The Chinese have always used it for a variety of storage chests.

Other valuable species of **Cinnamomum** include **C. zeylanicum,** the Ceylon Cinnamon, principal source of the popular spice; **C. burmanii,** the Padang Cinnamon, an inferior source of the same spice; **C. cassia,** the Chinese Cassia, source of both cassia and cinnamon; and **C. loureirii,** the Saigon Cinnamon, raised for the same purpose.

A particularly interesting feature of all the Cinnamon trees is that the volatile oils they contain are attractive to butterflies, which spend a great deal of time hovering about the foliage.

Cinnamomum burmanii
Padang Cinnamon

Citharexylum quadrangulare
Jamaica Fiddlewood

CITHAREXYLUM

Fiddlewood
* **Evergreen /fast**
* **Golden leaf colour**
* **Ht: to 17m /50ft**

Closely related both to the shrubby Lantana and the annual Verbena, Fiddlewoods or **Citharexylum** are a small genus of dainty trees from South America and the Caribbean area. They are immensely popular in warm and temperate climates worldwide.

The most commonly seen species is probably **C. quadrangulare,** the Jamaica Fiddlewood, a handsome, glossy-leafed tree valued principally for its colour in the cool winter garden, when the foliage turns a delightful golden bronze. Its branches and twigs are rectangular in section; the 10cm leaves are long and pointed, without teeth. Small, white five-petalled flowers appear in spring.

Fiddlewood timber is regarded as a useful cabinet wood in its native zone.

Citrus aurantium
Valencia Orange

Citrus X 'Tangelo'
Seminole Tangelo

Citrus aurantiifolia
Tahiti Lime

CITRUS

Oranges and Lemons
* **Evergreen/slow**
* **Winter fruits**
* **Ht: 3-5m/10-15ft**

All 15-odd **Citrus** species and their innumerable varieties are native to South-East Asia, and it seems likely that the first of them arrived in Europe with the Moorish invaders of the Middle Ages.

Since then they have been highly valued for their fragrant and volatile oils, and for the gorgeously coloured fruits, which ripen in winter from the previous spring's flowers. At least, that is what they do in the right climate. In cooler areas they may not ripen until the following summer.

Most **Citrus** trees are happy with an outdoor winter temperature as low as 7°C/45°F, though they have been known to resist short frosty spells, particularly Oranges.

Most commonly grown **Citrus** are hybrids of several original species. These include:

C. aurantiifolia (Lime) green, ovoid fruit.
C. aurantium (Seville Orange), sour fruit.
C. decumana (Pomelo) 15cm yellow fruits.
C. limon (Lemon) ovoid yellow fruit; spiny.
C. medica (Citron) 25cm gold fruit.
C. X paradisii (Grapefruit) Pomelo X orange.
C. reticulata (Mandarin) flattened fruit.
C. sinensis (Sweet Orange) Most common.
C. X tangelo (Pomelo X Mandarin cross).

Citrus grow best in a moist, humid atmosphere, and are often used in coastal areas or by large rivers. In any event they appreciate a daily spray of the foliage in dry weather, which also keeps at bay the innumerable pests attracted by their volatile leaf-oils. They like a deep rich soil, but with some sand for drainage, and plenty of manure and other fertilizer during the growing season. They are propagated from buds of the chosen variety grafted onto seedling stock.

All **Citrus** species have the same dark glossy leaves, often with curiously bladed or winged leaf stalks. The white, or sometimes mauve-tinted flowers may appear at any time, but most heavily in spring. They are fragrant and most attractive to bees. The fruits may be yellow, orange, red or green according to variety, and vary from 2.5cm in diameter for the Calamondin to 22.5cm for the Pomelo and Citron.

Citrus limon
Eureka Lemon

Citrus reticulata
Mandarin Orange

COCCOLOBA

Sea Grape
* **Evergreen /fast**
* **Warm weather fruits**
* **Ht: to 7m /20ft**

T H

The Sea Grape, **Coccoloba uvifera,** was at one time used in place of writing paper by early settlers in Mexico. A very handsome tree, it is used throughout the world in tropical seaside gardens for its great salt resistance and the privacy afforded by its dense foliage.

Coccoloba is grown from cuttings and seeds, and rapidly reaches 7m in a warm position, the trunk thick and squat. The leaves are round and may reach 20cm across, giving the tree a popular name of Platter-leaf. At maturity, the leaves are thick and shiny, with distinct red veins. The small greenish-white flowers appear in dense racemes up to 25cm long, and are followed by strings of purplish-red fruits that are quite edible.

The hard timber takes a fine polish and is used for cabinet making in the West Indies. Other parts of the plant have a variety of medicinal uses.

Coccoloba uvifera
Sea Grape

Coffea arabica
Coffee

COFFEA

Coffee
* **Evergreen /fast**
* **Summer berries**
* **Ht: to 5m /15ft**

T

H

Rarely thought of as a tree, **Coffea arabica** is usually seen pruned to shrub height to make berry-picking easier. As the source of all the coffee we drink, it is obviously of great value in commerce, but grow it as an ornamental by all means if you live in a temperate climate. It has handsome, shiny leaves, like those of related **Gardenias,** and showy white spring blossom.

The green berries that follow turn a brilliant red. Each contains two seeds or beans that roasted, dried and ground make up your breakfast cup of coffee. Well, with another forty-one they do!

The name **Coffea** is an approximation of the original Arabic name for this plant.

CORNUS

Dogwood, Cornel
* **Deciduous /fast**
* **Autumn fruit /colour**
* **Ht: 8-20m /25-60ft**

I shall never forget my first train ride to Virginia, speeding on the Powhatan Arrow through the Allegheny mountains in the clear light of an April morning. All along the valley route, the landscape was touched with spring — dark coal-mining towns alternating with a riot of lime green foliage, fern and fuzz. And here and there against the drab rocks and brilliance of a million flowering dogwoods, white, pink and almost red.

It was only later, in a friend's garden in Roanoke, that I discovered the inflorescence of the common Flowering Dogwood **(Cornus florida)** is not a flower at all, but a whole composite head of tiny greenish flowers with four spectacularly marked bracts enclosing the group. When the bracts fall, the flowers develop into a cluster of bright red fruits which persist into autumn, joining the foliage in a fiery farewell to summer. **C. florida** is a slim, dark-trunked tree growing from 5 to 12m in height, its crepy, pointed leaves marked with conspicuous parallel veins.

There are around a hundred species of Dogwood found in cool-winter temperate parts of America and Asia, many of them shrubs with brilliantly coloured winter bark.

Other tree species of note include: **C. capitata,** a widely branched Himalayan tree of 15m and partly evergreen; the bracts are creamy-white, the fruit like a rather large raspberry. **C. controversa,** the Giant Dogwood from the Himalayas, grows to 20m; leaves whitish beneath, masses of pinkish flowers with cream bracts in summer. **C. kousa,** a small Japanese tree of 7m, deciduous, with dense masses of creamy-pink bracted blossoms in early summer. **C. mas,** the Cornelian Cherry, another small tree from Europe and Asia, deciduous, with yellow flowers and dark red edible fruits; it has many highly coloured leaf varieties.

Early missionaries in North America fancied a mystical connection between the inflorescence of the Dogwood and the crucifixion, since the four bracts, arranged in the form of a cross, each bore a marking like a nail hole.

Cornus florida
Dogwood, fruit

Cornus capitata
Himalayan Strawberry

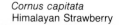

Crataegus succulentus
Colorado Thorn

Crataegus monogyna
Common Hawthorn

Crataegus ellwangeriana

CRATAEGUS

Hawthorn
* **Deciduous /fast**
* **Autumn fruits**
* **Ht: 5-15m /15-45ft** [C] [T]

Gives not the hawthorn bush a sweeter shade
Than doth a rich embroidered canopy?

Good old Shakespeare! As usual, he said it all in signalling his approval of the ubiquitous hedgerow tree of English fields, the Common Hawthorn or May, **Crataegus monogyna.**

Planted throughout the British Isles, its thorny branches burst into white clouds of tiny, sharp-scented, rose-like blossom in spring. The onset of frost reveals a blaze of autumn colour and a fine crop of red fruits that persist into winter.

Yet the Common Hawthorn is but one of perhaps a thousand species of these deciduous members of the rose family, found principally in North America, but with flourishing groups native to Europe, Asia Minor and North Africa.

They all prefer a cooler climate and are frost-hardy. Most of them have decorative foliage, either lobed or rose-like, frequently associated with the most vicious thorns in the botanical kingdom. The variations between them are principally in height of growth (ranging from 5 to 15m), and in size and colour of fruit, varying from currant-size to that of a small apple, in every shade of red, white and pink, and a few in orange and yellow.

The Mexican Thorn, **C. stipulacea,** has toothed, rose-like leaves and masses of large orange-yellow spotted fruits that hang on the tree for months. The American **C. submollis** has yellow fruits on long, hanging stems. **C. ellwangeriana** has scarlet apple-like fruits to 4cm wide. **C. crusgalli,** the Cockspur Thorn, has the longest, sharpest spines. And the hybrid **C. X smithiana** seems to combine the best of all possible worlds: fast growth, weeping habit, large flowers and enormous fruit clusters in a particularly glowing red.

All species grow easily from seed, which takes two years to ripen. Grafting is used for fancy varieties. **Crataegus** is from the Greek word *kratos,* meaning strength, referring to its hard wood.

Crataegus stipulacea
Mexican Thorn

Crataegus X *smithiana*
Hybrid Thorn

CRESCENTIA

Calabash Tree
* **Evergreen/fast**
* **Summer fruit**
* **Ht: to 13m/40ft** H

The tropical American tree **Crescentia cujete** is grown today solely as an ornamental, but in earlier times it was valued highly for the storage potential of its enormous woody-shelled fruit which can easily reach 30cm in diameter.

Primitive musicians found the hollow shells made sensational rattles, and they are still used by Afro-Cuban bands and Hawaiian hula groups.

Crescentia (named for the thirteenth century Italian botanist, Crescenzi) is a rather heavy tree with decorative grey bark and densely-foliaged spreading branches. The shiny leaves are blunt-ended. The greenish flowers open at night directly from the larger branches. There they are followed by the shining green Calabash fruit.

C. cujete is the only one of its genus.

Crescentia cujete
Calabash Tree

Cryptomeria japonica
Japanese Cedar

CRYPTOMERIA

Sugi, Japanese Cedar
* **Evergreen/fast** C
* **Decorative foliage**
* **Ht: to 50m/150ft** T

Cryptomeria is a Japanese coniferous genus, with only a single species (**C. japonica**) but a myriad foliage varieties.

In its normal form, it is a handsome, pyramidal tree growing as high as 50m in deep rich soil. Its stiff, scale-like leaves are arranged spirally in long tassels.

The fancy-leafed varieties are propagated from cuttings struck in a sandy medium under heat. They include: **albo-variegata,** with white-flecked leaves; **araucarioides** with slender branchlets; **bandai-sugi,** a broad-growing dwarf; **elegans,** with feathery foliage that turns bronze in autumn; **pendula,** with weeping branches; and **spiralis** with twisted branchlets.

Cryptomerias are suited to any cool or temperate climate.

Cunninghamia lanceolata
China Fir

CUNNINGHAMIA

China Fir
* **Evergreen /fast**
* **Summer cones**
* **Ht: 33-40m /100-120ft**

|T|

|H|

China's most indispensable tree, the tall and elegant **Cunninghamia,** is related to Japan's **Cryptomeria** (see previous entry), to the American Bald Cypress (see **Taxodium**) and to Australia's **Araucarias.**

It is a tall, fast-growing conifer reaching up to 35m and is found naturally only in China's southern provinces. Like the **Araucarias,** it is not at all cold-hardy, growing only at low altitudes of a subtropical climate.

The fragrant timber is easily worked and much sought-after for every purpose from house and boat building to the construction of coffins. The bark is scaly, red-brown and constantly peeling. The horizontally held branches are densely covered with two rows of spirally arranged, flattened needles, each

about 6cm long. In spring the China Fir bears inconspicuous flower clusters, both male and female. These mature into scaly cones about the size of a golf ball.

Like California's related **Sequoias,** the **Cunninghamias** have the remarkable ability to renew themselves readily after felling, by sending up new shoots from the base of the trunk. **C. lanceolata** is the Chinese species, and much cultivated in warmer areas of the United States, southern Europe and South America.

There are two other species, **C. kawakamii** from Taiwan, which grows to 35m and is rarely found in cultivation, and **C. konishii,** the similar Taiwan Fir. This has spirally arranged, stiff leaves 4cm in length, male flowers in a cluster, ovoid female cones to 2.5cm long. It is a fast-growing tree, ideal for subtropical gardens, but rarely seen outside South-East Asia.

The genus was named for James Cunningham, an early explorer of China.

CUPANIOPSIS

Tuckeroo
* **Evergreen**/fast [T]
* **Summer fruits**
* **Ht: to 13m/40ft** [H]

Evergreen, and native to Australia, the handsome Tuckeroo, **Cupaniopsis anacardioides** is one of about fifty species found only in the Western Pacific area.

Smooth and pale of bark, it may reach 13m in warmer areas. Its branches are clothed all year with heavy leaves, each consisting of about eight blunt-ended shiny green leaflets. Small white flowers are scarcely noticeable.

The Tuckeroo's real display is in midsummer, when the hanging clusters of 2cm orange-yellow fruits ripen. They are full of sticky red pulp and black seeds, believed to have been an Aboriginal delicacy.

The Tuckeroo has become popular in many countries with climates similar to the Australian east coast, and is much used as a street tree. It is of particular value in coastal areas, being salt-resistant.

Cupaniopsis anacardioides
Tuckeroo

Cupaniopsis
fruit

Cupressus sempervirens stricta
Italian Cypress

CUPRESSUS

Cypress
  * **Evergreen /fast**
  * **Foliage varieties**
  * **Ht: 17-50cm /50-150ft**

C

T

As the False Cypresses are to cooler climates (see **Chamaecyparis**), so the True Cypresses, **Cupressus,** are to the mild temperate garden — the most versatile and

varied group of coniferous plants. Native to Europe, America and parts of Asia, the twenty or more species vary astonishingly in habit of growth.

The classic types are the tall, pencil-shaped Italian Cypress of many Mediterranean landscapes, **C. sempervirens stricta;** and the craggy windblown effect of California's Monterey Cypress, **C. macrocarpa.** Somewhere in between are those with a wonderful weeping habit, including **C. funeb-**

Cupressus CV 'Swane's Golden'
Golden Pencil Pine

CUPRESSUS (continued)

ris, the Mourning Cypress from China, and **C. lusitanica,** the Mexican Weeping Cypress.

The Asiatic Bhutan Cypress, **C. torulosa,** from the western Himalayas, has very much the habit of the Cedars, pyramidal when young, but branching into a high crown in middle age.

Foliage colours may be blue-grey as in **C. glabra,** the Arizona Cypress, or bright golden yellow as in many of the coloured leaf varieties of **C. macrocarpa.**

As a general rule, the branchlets of True Cypresses are not held in flat planes like those of the False Cypress, and the leaves are modified into scales so tiny they can hardly be distinguished from the stems. The flowers are virtually invisible, and the scaly, globular cones hang on the trees for several years before splitting to release the seeds.

Very few of the Cypress genus are frost-hardy, and all do best in warm sheltered positions. They are generally raised from seed (except of course the fancy coloured types), but cuttings will strike if taken in late autumn. Cypresses should be planted as small as possible, for larger specimens do not transplant well.

Cupressus macrocarpa 'Brunoniana'
Golden Cypress

Cupressus glabra
Arizona Cypress

CYDONIA

Quince
* **Deciduous/slow**
* **Autumn fruits**
* **Ht: 7m/20ft**   C   T

More popular before refrigeration, when it lasted well into winter, the delicious Quince is little more than a rose hip, blown up to a diameter of 12.5cm and more. Botanically **Cydonia oblonga,** it is native to eastern Europe and western Asia and has been cultivated since time immemorial.

The tree is deciduous, with leaves rather like those of an apple. It may reach 7m and is usually of a rather shrubby appearance unless pruned. The flowers are perfumed and charming.

The great, irregularly shaped fruits ripen in autumn, persisting on the tree after leaves have yellowed and fallen.

Quinces cannot be eaten raw, but can be stewed with honey or sugar. The rather grainy-textured flesh cooks up a brilliant scarlet-pink, looking and tasting most appetizing.

Cydonia oblonga
Quince

Dacrydium cupressinum
Rimu

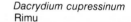

DACRYDIUM

Rimu
* **Evergreen/slow**   C
* **Decorative, weeping**
* **Ht: to 25m/80ft**   T

Surprisingly few of New Zealand's remarkable trees are seen in cultivation outside that country. One notable exception is the Rimu or Red Pine, **Dacrydium cupressinum,** a favourite specimen tree in cool, frost-free areas throughout the world.

The Rimu is a slow-growing conifer which may ultimately reach a height of 25m in ideal conditions, but is not likely to exceed a third of that in an average lifetime. The foliage consists of tiny scale-like leaves which overlap along the length of long, weeping branchlets.

The botanical name **Dacrydium** is a diminutive form of the ancient Greek word for a tear — an allusion not to the weeping habit, but to sparkling drops of gum exuded by the tree's fruit.

Diospyros kaki
Persimmon

DIOSPYROS

Persimmon, Date Plum, Kaki
* **Deciduous /fast**
* **Autumn fruit, colour**
* **Ht: to 13m /40ft**

C T

Tricky to eat, the luscious fruit of the Persimmon **(Diospyros kaki)** can all but paralyse the tongue unless they have reached the exact stage of squashy ripeness when their astringent principle is converted to sugary sweetness.

A strikingly handsome tree, the Persimmon flourishes anywhere from the subtropics to cool temperate zones. It may reach 13m in old age, but is limited to half that in the average garden. The trunk is picturesque and twisted, the branches trailing the ground in some of the named varieties. Oval 18cm leaves turn on a magnificent show as the cold weather approaches: orange, scarlet, even imperial purple. The small yellowish flowers are merely a necessary stage toward the gorgeous tomato-sized fruits that follow. These persist on the branches well into winter, if you can be persuaded to leave them alone.

Persimmons grow from seed but the best varieties are propagated by grafting.

Diospyros virginiana
Possumwood

Diospyros kaki
Persimmon, fruit

DURIO

Durian, King of Fruits
* **Evergreen /fast**
* **Summer fruit**
* **Ht: to 20m /60ft** H

Though the remarkable **Durio zibethinus** will not grow away from the tropics, its fruit is something of a legend. 'Tastes like heaven,' say the Chinese, 'but smells like hell.' The specific epithet **zibethinus** means 'smelling like a civet, or tomcat'. It is, needless to say, an acquired taste, but a taste acquired by Chinese everywhere (to them it is 'King of Fruits') and by millions of Western tourists.

The tree is large, with a heavily buttressed trunk, the leaves simple and slightly oblong. Clusters of 5cm white flowers appear directly from the branches, followed by heavy football-sized spiny fruits. The creamy pulp is the edible part, and I can assure you, does taste delicious. The fruit is sometimes available at Chinese stores, both fresh and canned.

Durio zibethinus
Durian

Eriobotrya japonica
Loquat

ERIOBOTRYA

Loquat, Japanese Medlar
* **Evergreen /fast**
* **Winter fruits**
* **Ht: to 8m /25ft** T H

Raised in temperate to tropical climates for its succulent winter fruits, the Loquat, **Eriobotrya japonica,** is a small tree, rarely above 7m in height. It is related to other fruiting trees of the rose family, and the rather brittle dark foliage is evergreen and woolly beneath. Small five-petalled flowers appear in autumn, the fruits ripen at various times in winter according to variety and location. The size of a pingpong ball, slightly oval and a pale apricot in colour, they are very succulent, with a sweetly acid flavour, and enclose several large slippery seeds.

The Loquat is native to China and southern Japan, and is popular in southern Europe, southern and western USA, Australia, Africa and many other places.

Eucalyptus mannifera
Red-spotted Gum

EUCALYPTUS

Gum Tree, Eucalypt
* **Evergreen /fast**
* **All year**
* **Ht: 8-50m /25-150ft**

C

T H

In Australia, the ubiquitous Gum Tree is king. To all points of the compass, and in the central desert, the great bulk of the continent's natural tree-life consists of one or another of the 600 and more recorded species of **Eucalyptus.** Often very localized by species,

the Gums as a group are highly adaptable, and in fact astonishingly adapted to the rigours of life in many diverse climates.

Some species flourish in swamps, others eke out a sparse existence in barren deserts where the rainfall in one year may be nil. There are low, scrubby, many-trunked types in the sandplains, tall needle-straight giants in the forests of Western Australia, Victoria and Tasmania, some of them (**E. regnans,** the Mountain Ash) arguably the tallest trees on earth!

The great River Red Gums send out a

EUCALYPTUS (continued)

labyrinth of roots near water, helping combat erosion; the gnarled and hardy Snow Gums twist and sprawl on the lee side of mountains high above the snowline.

The Eucalypts have become Australia's most influential export, used for reafforestation in many of the world's most barren areas which often (but wrongly) imagine them to be their own. With very few exceptions, all the world's Eucalypts have originated from Australian seed in the last century.

The exceptions which have not originated in Australia are a few tropic species spread over islands as far north as the southern Philippines. The particularly decorative Mindinao Gum **(E. deglupta)** from the Philippines is grown in many parts of the Pacific.

Eucalypts yield several valuable oils, and because of the enormous quantities of flowers they bear, are an important source of honey. The timber of many species provides some of the best hardwoods in the world. The New South Wales Blackbutt has a timber so hard and strong that it was used as load-bearing columns of buildings up to six storeys in height in earlier days.

Eucalypt bark may be smooth and paper-thin (as in **E. citriodora,** the Lemon-scented Gum), or rough and deeply fissured as in the many Stringybarks and Ironbarks. The leaves vary widely according to species both in length and in width, ranging all the way from spear-shaped to heart-shaped, with often a recognizably different leafshape in juvenile foliage, which makes them very tricky to identify.

Eucalypts are usually grown from seed, and accordingly their flower colours and leaf-shapes are notoriously unstable. They are fast growers in garden conditions, and grow quicker from small seedlings than from larger nursery-bought plants.

In common with many other Australian plants, they resent cultivation in their vicinity. They have one peculiarity of growth which is virtually unique in the tree world. This is the lignotuber, a vast bulb-like growth which develops just below ground level in many species. It serves as a storage chamber for many plant nutrients and allows the tree to survive a dry season or even regenerate completely after devastating fires have destroyed all above-ground growth.

Eucalyptus globulus
Tasmanian Blue Gum

Eucalyptus pauciflora
Snow Gum

Eucalyptus citriodora
Lemon-scented Gum

Eucalyptus camaldulensis
River Red Gum

Eucalyptus deglupta
Mindinao Gum

64

EUPHORIA

Loong Ngan,
Dragon's Eye
* **Evergreen/fast**
* **Summer fruit**
* **Ht: 13m/40ft**

T H

One of Asia's most popular trees, the Loong Ngan is only known in the West as the source of a delicious canned fruit sometimes served in Chinese restaurants.

The Loong Ngan can be grown over a wide range, being somewhat resistant to frost and needing protection from the full tropical sun in summer.

Its handsome foliage consists of compound leaves with up to twelve pointed leaflets each, often highly coloured when young. The tiny yellow flowers appear both at the end of twigs and at the leaf bases.

The fruits are smooth and about the size of a grape, greenish at first, but taking on a red tint as they ripen. They may be eaten fresh, preserved or dried. The original Chinese name, Loong Ngan or Dragon's Eye has been incorporated into the botanical name **Euphoria longan.**

The Loong Ngan can be propagated from seed, half-ripened cuttings or layers. It needs a deep, compost-rich soil and regular fertilizing when developing fruit.

Euphoria longan
Loong-Ngan

Fagus sylvatica
Beechnuts

FAGUS

Beech
C
* **Deciduous/fast**
* **Autumn nuts**
T
* **Ht: 30-40m/90-120ft**

Found only in limited areas of the temperate Northern Hemisphere, the Beeches (**Fagus** spp.) include some of the biggest and most beloved of cool-climate deciduous trees — in particular, the many fancy-leafed varieties of the European Beech, **F. sylvatica.**

Beeches are deciduous and generally possessed of that most sought-after of qualities, a preference for lime-rich, chalky soils. Provided there is good drainage, they romp ahead, growing to 30m and reproducing rapidly from fallen seed. Left to themselves they soon form a Beech forest, for with their

Fagus sylvatica asplenifolia
Fern-leaf Beech

FAGUS (continued)

dense leaf canopies and surface-foraging roots, nothing else will grow in the vicinity.

European **F. sylvatica** is a graceful tree, tall and slim in woodland conditions, widely spreading as a specimen, often with weeping branches. The prominently veined leaves are almost translucent and covered with fine, silky hair. Their shape is a perfect pointed oval, and the colour may vary from the normal green towards either gold or purple according to variety. There are also variegated cultivars and several with finely toothed and lobed leaves.

After a relatively insignificant flower display, the Beeches develop a crop of small triangular nuts enclosed in spiny-hairy cases which split open in autumn. These Beechnuts are relatively flavourless to humans, but a great success with pigs. The timber is popular in furniture making.

The related American Beech **(F. grandifolia)** is also an important timber tree in that country, but not grown much elsewhere. Its leaves are larger and coarsely serrated.

In Japan they grow the native **F. crenata.**

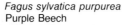

Fagus sylvatica purpurea
Purple Beech

Fagus sylvatica
Common Beech

FICUS

Figs and Banyans
* **Evergreen /fast**
* **Summer fruits**
* **Ht: 10-70m /30-200ft** [T] [H]

How curious that the enormous genus that includes some of the world's largest trees should be known collectively by the name of its least spectacular member. **Ficus** was the name the Romans gave to the generally small, shrubby Fig tree from Asia Minor, whose leaves the Bible tells us were worn by Adam and Eve. But both popular and botanical names stuck when its gigantic cousins were discovered later in many tropical parts of the world. Certainly the other trees, towering constructions with aerial roots and strangling branches, don't look much like the Figs of our orchards, so why are they classed in the same genus?

As is so often the case, it's a matter of the flowers. You will never see a Fig tree of any sort in flower. They produce only small hollow receptacles closed with a miniscule flapped opening or ostiole. The even more minute flowers are borne inside this receptacle. When fertilized by a small wasp the receptacle ripens into a generally pear-shaped, rather squashy fruit.

The Common Fig, **F. carica,** is also the exception in being deciduous, and in bearing rough-textured, three-lobed leaves. Almost

Ficus retusa
Chinese Banyan

Ficus benjamina
Weeping Banyan

Ficus carica
Common Fig

Ficus macrophylla
Moreton Bay Fig

Ficus religiosa
Bo Tree

FICUS (continued)

all the others are evergreen with handsome shiny leaves, ranging from 2.5 to 30cm in length. Many of these are among the most reliable and popular of indoor plants, but in that form scarcely hint at their tropical grandeur.

While **F. benjamina** for instance (the Weeping Laurel or Chinese Banyan) is a dainty little weeping plant indoors, I have seen them in Hawaii over 35m in diameter and almost half that in height, or hanging their long, weeping branches 17m down toward the Brisbane River. They adore humidity and should not be grown in dry areas.

F. lyrata, the Fiddleleaf or Banjo Fig that sprouts its rough, guitar-shaped leaves in many an apartment, reaches 15m in the Philippines or its native Africa.

And there is the ubiquitous **F. elastica** or India Rubber Tree. One tree in Assam is said to have grown 37m in just over thirty years — a good reason for not planting out your pet indoor plant when it gets too big!

The Banyan **(F. benghalensis),** also from India, sends down aerial roots from its branches which develop into new, supporting trunks wherever they touch ground, soon forming a dense forest. One famous Banyan in India is almost 1km in circumference.

Australia's Moreton Bay Fig **(F. macrophylla)** has been reported to 70m in the wild while its look-alike Port Jackson or Rusty Fig, **F. rubiginosa,** rarely reaches 20m. It is common in the Sydney area, has brown leaf reverses, often forms secondary trunks from aerial roots.

F. religiosa, the Peepul or Bo Tree beneath which Buddha meditated, can grow gigantic. It bears fluttering, heart-shaped leaves that tremble, it is said, remembering the Buddha's divine thoughts.

F. microcarpa CV 'Hillii' is a small-leafed giant, popular in the United States as **F. retusa nitida.**

F. sycamorus from Africa is the Sycamore of the Bible, and bears its fruit on masses of small leafless twigs.

There are over 600 known **Ficus** species. Though many of them are popularly known as rubber trees, and their sticky sap can be tapped and processed into latex, they are not the trees of commercial rubber plantations. Those are **Hevea brasiliensis,** a different species altogether.

Fraxinus X 'Raywoodii'
Claret Ash

FRAXINUS

Ash Tree
* **Deciduous /fast**
* **Autumn colour**
* **Ht: 10-45cm /30-140ft** C T

One of the most widely grown genera of largely deciduous trees from the Northern Hemisphere, the **Fraxinus** or Ashes have a wide climatic range spreading from quite frosty areas into hill climates of the tropics. There are over sixty species found in nature on all three continents, and many fancy cultivated varieties, particularly of the European Ash **(F. excelsior).**

As a genus, they are most variable in size, ranging from a small shrubby build to giants of 50m and more. With very few exceptions they are resistant to all extremes of weather, provided the soil is deep and rich.

Their trademark is a foliage of decorative pinnate leaves, rarely more than 30cm long, and consisting of from three to thirteen leaflets, lightly toothed and with the odd one borne on the end. The small flowers appear in dense clusters, generally before the leaves, in early spring. Later, they develop into a mass of small samaras or seeds that hang on the end of branches, each like a single, flattened wing. These are quite showy, especially in the Mediterranean

69

FRAXINUS (continued)

species **F. ornus** or Manna Ash.

Particularly popular in cultivation are: the Golden Ash (**F. excelsior** CV 'Aurea') which produces handsome golden-green leaves that colour brilliantly in autumn; the Weeping Ash **(F. excelsior pendula)**, a very heavy tree with branches that not only hang down, but run along the ground; **F.** X 'Raywoodii', the Claret Ash, an Australian-raised hybrid that colours a wonderful deep red-bronze in autumn; the evergreen Mexican Ash **(F. uhdei)**; and the spectacular White Ash **(F. americana)** from the eastern United States, that colours vividly in autumn with a distinct touch of mauve among the gold.

All Ashes grow readily from seed, which should be stored until spring and heat-treated before sowing. They are valuable timber trees, and popular everywhere for street planting.

Fraxinus uhdei
Mexican Evergreen Ash

Fraxinus spp.
Ash Trees

Fraxinus ornus
Manna Ash

GINKGO

Maidenhair Tree
* **Deciduous /slow**
* **Autumn colour /**
  summer fruits
* **Ht: to 40m /120ft**

C

T

The graceful **Ginkgo** is the Rip Van Winkle of botany — a tree lost in time and suddenly revived into a world changed beyond recognition.

If that hyperbole sounds melodramatic, the facts are even more so. **Ginkgo** (and other trees very similar to it in the same family) first flourished in Europe and Asia, in Australia and even in America, some 200 million years ago. The leaves have been found again and again in fossil strata from the Palaeozoic era when the earth was a jungle of steamy swamps. It was known to scientists for centuries as the ancestor of all conifers, but believed quite extinct. And so we believe it still to be, that is, in the wild. But in the gardens of certain remote and ancient Chinese temples, it lived on. The Western world first heard of it in the seventeenth century, and actually saw it in 1730 when the first living specimen was imported by Dutch traders. And so, the **Ginkgo** began life all over again, reconquering its former range, country by country.

For a tree from so ancient and tranquil a background, it does better in city conditions than almost any modern tree. Throughout polluted Tokyo you see it fresh and green, growing on some of the world's most choked and busy thoroughfares.

Ginkgo biloba is cold-hardy, but loves summer heat. It is quite immune to disease, fast-growing and can cope with either dry or wet conditions. It may be propagated from seed or by layering or grafting. **Gingko** may grow to 40m in a warm climate, but around a third of that is more normal. The leaves closely resemble the Maidenhair Fern to which it owes its popular name, although the Chinese, more practically, call it the 'Duck's Foot Tree'.

On one old **Ginkgo** tree in the Tokyo Botanic Gardens, I noticed a curious feature to which I have not found reference elsewhere. These were a series of hanging protuberances like stalactites or pendulous breasts. Their purpose is a mystery to me.

Ginkgo biloba
Ginkgo

Ginkgo
autumn foliage

Gleditsia triacanthos
Honey Locust

Gleditsia CV 'Sunburst'

GLEDITSIA

Honey Locust
 * **Deciduous /fast**   C
 * **Autumn colour**
 * **Ht: 12-50m /36-150ft**   T

I find it very difficult to remember the correct botanical name for a plant when I can't even pronounce or spell it. **Eschscholzia** for instance. Surely there was a naturalist with an easier name by which to remember the lovely California Poppy?

And why name a wonderful genus of trees after a man named Gleditsch, even if he was once director of the Berlin Botanical Garden?

Fortunately, reason has at last prevailed, and the name has now been mercifully simplified to **Gleditsia,** which identifies a small genus of trees in the pea family, Leguminosae, found only in Asia and North America. Small the genus may be, but very distinctive, widely planted as street and specimen trees all over the temperate world, both dry and wet.

Most commonly seen is the North American Honey Locust, **G. triacanthos,** which is deciduous and grows as tall as 50m in its native land, though much less elsewhere. It produces bipinnate leaves with up to thirty-two leaflets, small green pea flowers in furry racemes and masses of sickle-shaped pea pods up to 45cm long. But its most noticeable feature is the barrier of wickedly branched spines that emerge in clusters all over the trunk. Indeed a difficult tree to climb, but how much worse to descend! Its gold-leafed cultivar 'Sunburst' is particularly decorative.

The Japanese species **G. japonica** is very similar though barely half the size, and with very corkscrew-twisted pods.

The Persian **G. caspica** has a very warty trunk and much smaller pods.

The Chinese **G. sinensis** is similar to the Japanese type, though smaller, and with untwisted purplish pods.

All **Gleditsias** grow easily from seed, and curiously for members of the pea family, are both frost and drought-hardy. Their pods, filled with sweetish pulp, are edible, hence the popular name of Honey Locust.

72

Gleditsia triacanthos
spine detail

Harpephyllum caffrum
Kaffir Plum

Harpephyllum
fruit detail

HARPEPHYLLUM

Kaffir Plum
* **Evergreen /fast**
* **Summer fruit**
* **Ht: to 10m /30ft**

Very much a loner, South Africa's distinctive Kaffir Plum, **Harpephyllum caffrum,** is rarely seen naturally in the company of other plants, for its dense canopy of foliage prevents any rain at all from reaching below its branches. Dark and glossy at a distance, it is widely cultivated in temperate climates, as both street and specimen tree.

On close inspection, the compound leaves are handsome and Ash-like, consisting of a number of shiny, pointed leaflets, each 7cm in length.

The fairly insignificant green flowers open in spring, and are followed by neat little clusters of fruit, nestling like a clutch of eggs in the dense foliage at branch tips. These are oval, and about the size of Cumquats. They ripen from green, through scarlet, to a rich purple, and can be made into a delicious conserve.

73

Harpullia pendula
Tulipwood

Harpullia arborea
Philippine Tulipwood

HARPULLIA

Tulipwood
* **Deciduous /fast**
* **Summer fruits**
* **Ht: 12-17m /36-50ft**

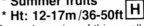

Several species of this small group of trees, native to South-East Asia, Australia and nearby islands, are cultivated in moist, warm-climate areas. They are valued as street or specimen trees, and also for magnificent brown and yellow streaked timber.

Most commonly seen is **Harpullia pendula,** a 15m inhabitant of Australia's warm east coastal forests. It has striking Ash-like compound leaves and the most curious bright orange fruits or pods. Each one consists of a pair of globular capsules joined together like a dumb-bell and containing two shiny black seeds. As they mature, the paired pods split open and look for all the world like the disembodied eyes of some sinister doll. Doll's Eyes is in fact one of its popular names, Tulipwood another.

HETEROMELES

California Holly, Toyon
* **Evergreen/fast**
* **Autumn berries** [T]
* **Ht: to 10m/30ft**

Without California's ubiquitous Toyon, there wouldn't be a Hollywood. For the cinema city was so named because of the widely spreading groves of this colourfully fruited tree which reminded early settlers of the cold-climate Hollies.

Alas, the groves of California Holly have now disappeared beneath a landscape of neon and concrete, and the sturdy trees have emigrated to gardens in many other temperate parts of the world.

Heteromeles arbutifolia grows to 10m, has leathery elliptical leaves and often needs a bit of help from the secateurs to look more like a tree, less like a bushy shrub.

It can be propagated from seeds, cuttings or layers, is hardy in cool frost-free areas, and grown both in Great Britain and New Zealand. Birds just love the berries.

Heteromeles arbutifolia
California Holly

Homalanthus populifolius
Bleeding Heart Tree

HOMALANTHUS

Bleeding Heart Tree,
Queensland Poplar
* **Evergreen/fast**
* **Grown for foliage**
* **Ht: to 5m/15ft** [C] [T] [H]

Found naturally from Ceylon to southern Australia and out into the Pacific Islands, the ubiquitous 'Bleeding Heart Tree', **Homalanthus populifolius,** seems to spring up anywhere, presumably from bird-borne seeds. It is an unobtrusive, lightly branched tree, rarely exceeding 5m in height, with handsome, velvety, heart-shaped leaves, 7.5 to 20cm in length. These are generally evergreen, but at any time of the year, some of them will turn bright red and hang on the tree like bleeding hearts, before dropping. Racemes of small yellowish flowers appear in summer — the two sexes borne separately, though on the same tree. The female flower clusters are long-stemmed, the male short. Greenish fruits about 1cm in diameter are attractive to birds only.

IDESIA

Wonder Tree, ligiri
* **Deciduous/fast**
* **Autumn berries**
* **Ht: 13m/40ft**

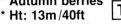

One of the world's most handsome berry trees, striking Chinese **Idesia polycarpa** can be relied on to preserve its bounty right through the cold months into spring, for birds don't seem to be interested in the fruit at all. The only catch is that you really need both a male and female tree to get a display in the first place.

Idesia is fast-growing to 13m in height and deciduous, bearing toothed, heart-shaped leaves that may reach 25cm long, and hang from reddish stems. The tiny greenish flowers hang in panicles, and on female trees develop into loose clusters of grape-sized berries. These are green at first, ripening through brown to a deep red.

Idesia can be propagated from seeds, cuttings or root-cuttings, and transplants well any time. It is commonly known as the Wonder Tree, but in Japan as ligiri.

Idesia polycarpa
Wonder Tree

Ilex opaca
American Holly

ILEX

Holly
* **Evergreen/slow**
* **Winter berries**
* **Ht: 7-25m/20-75ft**

It is easy to understand why Hollies exerted an almost mystical attraction to the peoples of Europe during the Middle Ages. When forests were bare of leaves, the ground blanketed in snow, there were the shiny pyramids of Holly catching winter sunlight with masses of brilliantly glossy fruit.

They were sacred to many of the old pagan gods, and even after Christianity came, the Holly still played its part in cheerful Yuletide decorations in honour of our Lord's birthday. What else was there to use, in those bleak winters?

Botanically speaking, the Holly is called **Ilex** (an old Roman name) and the European species **I. aquifolium** with pointed leaves is only one of about four hundred recognized species, native to almost every part of the

ILEX (continued)

world except Australasia. They are found mostly in colder areas of the Northern Hemisphere, and by no means all of them have spiny leaves.

To be sure of the winter berry crop, it is necessary to have trees of both sexes or a specially grafted specimen. Unfortunately, several of the most handsomely variegated species are exclusively male, can be propagated only from cuttings and will never bear fruit at all.

Hollies are best planted in very early autumn so they can make root growth before the cold weather. They like a sheltered but sunny position, and in warmer countries mostly prefer hill climates.

I. aquifolium grows into a magnificent pyramidal tree 25m in height, but not in an average lifetime, for it is a slow grower. The fancy-leafed varieties are perhaps more commonly seen, for they make a better display when not actually in fruit.

In other lands, other species are more popular, and there is a great range to choose from. The Japanese like **I. pedunculata,** the Mount Fuji Holly, with smooth-edged leaves and the berries hanging on long stems. The Chinese Holly **I. rotunda** is more popular in China and Hong Kong. It is a large, picturesquely gnarled tree of 20m with leathery leaves and masses of berries lasting well into spring. The American **I. opaca** is widely seen in the United States and Canada, where it is hardy in the bleak American winter. It grows

Ilex X 'Golden King'
Variegated Holly

Ilex pedunculata
Mount Fuji Holly

Ilex paraguariensis
Yerba Mate

Inocarpus edulis
Polynesian Chestnut

ILEX (continued)

about half the height of the European species. South America's favourite, **I. paraguariensis,** the Paraguay Tea or Yerba Mate, rarely exceeds 5m; a popular tea-like beverage is prepared from its dried leaves.

Hollies can be propagated from seed, or in the case of fancy varieties, from grafted buds or cuttings.

INOCARPUS

Polynesian Chestnut, Mape
* **Evergreen /fast**
* **Summer fruit**
* **Ht: 20m /60ft**   H

A valuable evergreen tree from Tahiti and neighbouring islands, the Mape or Polynesian Chestnut, **Inocarpus edulis,** has close relatives only in Indonesia, reinforcing some theories of early Polynesian migration. A tall, handsome tree of humid valleys and moist swampy areas, it develops a straight trunk with elaborately fluted buttresses. The leathery leaves are dark green, oblong, borne alternately, and most appetizing to stock. Since the introduction of European domestic animals, whole forests of them have been stripped of foliage to a considerable height.

The winter flowers are small, fragrant and white, appearing from the leaf axils. They are followed in spring by fibrous 5cm pods of a pale orange colour. These each contain one large seed or nut which, when cooked, becomes a delicacy with all the flavour and goodness of the European Chestnut, or as some would say, toasted almonds.

The clear sap turns scarlet on contact with the air, and has been used as a natural colouring for foods and artists' paints. It is also used as an astringent, and a lotion to ease the pain of jellyfish stings.

The Latin generic name **Inocarpus** means fibrous fruit and the specific name **edulis** means edible.

The Mape is propagated from half-ripened cuttings, but outside Tahiti and its neighbours I have seen it only in Hawaiian and Philippine gardens.

It is very fast growing, particularly in ill-drained swampy areas where it sucks up moisture to convert it into magnificent timber.

Inocarpus edulis
Mape

JUGLANS

Walnut [C]
* **Deciduous/slow** [T]
* **Summer nuts**
* **Ht: 15-50m/45-150ft**

The Romans thought so highly of these splendid trees and their delicious nuts that they named them in honour of the King of all their Gods, Jupiter's Acorn, or in Latin, *jovis glans,* which has come down to us as **Juglans,** the present botanic name.

The tree they knew in Rome was **J. regia,** the Common Walnut, a native of Persia, and it is believed this had been brought to Europe with the returning armies of Alexander the Great. It is still the best species, both for nuts and for the beautifully grained and patterned timber.

The Persian Walnut grows slowly to as high as 35m, but not in a single lifetime. It is deciduous, bearing spicily fragrant compound leaves with up to thirteen leaflets, and flowers in small greenish catkins. The oval, pointed nut ripens in a greenish husk, which ultimately sloughs away.

The American Walnut, **J. nigra,** is native to the eastern United States, and a much larger tree, reaching 50m at maturity, and very nearly as much across. Everything about it is larger: the leaves are longer and the fruit heavier and rounder (though not, gourmets insist, as tasty). It is most highly valued as a timber tree.

A Californian species **J. hindsii** is much grown in the western United States as a garden specimen or street tree. Rarely passing 15m in height, its compound leaves may have as many as 19 leaflets and its nuts are only half the size of the above species.

Other Walnuts are found in Japan, China, the Caribbean and South America.

J. regia, like others of the genus, is most readily propagated from the fresh nuts themselves, provided you get to them before the squirrels do. I had one in a Melbourne garden, many years ago, and had a fine crop of young plants every year, thanks to a forgetful squirrel which so busied itself all summer burying the nuts, that it was unable to locate them when it returned from winter quarters.

Juglans regia
Common Walnut Tree

Juglans regia
Walnuts

Juniperus chinensis torulosa
Hollywood Juniper

Juniperus CV 'Cologreen'
Colorado Red Cedar

JUNIPERUS

Juniper
  * **Evergreen /fast**
  * **Aromatic cones**
  * **Ht: 12-25m /35-75ft**

Scattered about all continents of the Northern Hemisphere, particularly in areas with generally alkaline soil, are the slow-growing Junipers, one of the most widespread of the coniferous genera.

There are more than fifty species, some of them with enough cultivated varieties to fill a large garden on their own.

Junipers are immensely popular for landscaping effect, and rightly so, for they thrive best in places where other lime-hating conifers cannot cope at all.

They are generally smaller trees than the related Cypresses and False Cypresses, except in their original species, which are rarely raised in gardens anyway. These include the Chinese Juniper, **Juniperus chinensis,** which may touch 20m, has many foliage and habit varieties, and needle-like juvenile foliage. Its cultivar 'Torulosa' with spirally twisted branches is known as the Hollywood Juniper.

The Common Juniper, **J. communis,** is found all over the Northern Hemisphere, rarely reaching 10m; it has sharply-pointed leaves and bluish berry-like cones. **J. sabina bermudiana** grows slowly to 13m, dragging heavy, lower branches on the ground. Its foliage is blue-grey, with blue cones 1cm in diameter. The Colorado Red Cedar, **J. scopulorum,** is again only 10m. The largest of all, **J. virginiana,** the Red Cedar, has been recorded at 25m and is raised commercially for pencil casings. Most popularly grown species is the dwarf **J. horizontalis** or Creeping Cedar, which is beloved of modern landscape gardeners and not a tree at all.

Adult Junipers have tiny scale-like leaves, like the True Cypress, and bear plump berry-like cones which may last on the tree for years. These are used all over the world to flavour gin.

Juniperus is the original Roman name for the genus. The species all grow readily from seed cones, which remain viable for years; the fancy-leafed varieties are propagated from cuttings.

KALOPANAX

Ivy Tree, Tree Aralia
* **Deciduous/fast**
* **Autumn colour**
* **Ht: to 25m/80ft**

C

T

A real Chinese puzzle of a tree, Asiatic **Kalopanax pictus** is closely related to Ivy, Aralia, Fatsia and many other popular houseplants, and has lookalike features in common with all of them. Question: just how do you design a tree to make all of these features fit together? First of all, you give it handsome 5-7 lobed leaves that look like ivy enlarged to a diameter of 30cm (even larger on young trees). Add late summer puffball clusters of small greenish flowers like those of Aralia. Follow with 4mm wide blue-black fruits like those of the Fatsia. Stick them all together on a tall, handsome tree that may grow to 25m high, and arm the trunk with stout spines to prevent anyone climbing up to take your handiwork apart. Foliage turns a rich gold in autumn.

Kalopanax pictus
Tree Aralia

Larix decidua
European Larch

LARIX

Larch
* **Deciduous/fast**
* **Autumn colour**
* **Ht: 27-50m/80-160ft**

C

Popular conifers for reafforestation in cold winter parts of the world, the Larches are no gloomy evergreens, like their cousins the Pines and Firs and Spruces, but charming lacy trees that celebrate every season with a brand new outfit.

In spring, the long weeping branchlets are clad with a lime-green fuzz of new needles; in autumn they turn a glowing gold and brown; and finally in winter, their spidery web of twigs and branchlets is decked with small brown cones, like tiny wooden roses.

There are ten species in the botanical genus **Larix.** All are fairly similar, except in size. The European Larch **(L. decidua)** has been measured to 50m in forests of central Europe, whereas the American Larch **(L. larcina)** rarely exceeds 20m.

LAURUS

Sweet Bay Tree
* **Evergreen/slow**
* **Spring flowers/**
  summer berries
* **Ht: to 13m/40ft**

What do the bay leaves in your kitchen have in common with the Laurel wreaths that crowned triumphant Roman heroes? They are identical — both being the leathery, fragrant foliage of the Sweet Bay Tree, **Laurus nobilis,** that grows throughout southern Europe.

So often do we see the Bay clipped to within an inch of its life that we sometimes forget it is in nature a handsome tree of up to 17m and more, crowned with its own dense wreaths of deep, glossy-green leaves. In spring the entire tree is decked with sprays of tiny greenish-yellow, four-petalled flowers, followed by shiny black berries.

Laurus is easily propagated from half-ripened cuttings, and deserves a place in any garden. *Laurus* was its original Roman name.

Laurus nobilis
Sweet Bay Tree

Leptospermum laevigatum
Coastal Tea Tree

LEPTOSPERMUM

Tea Tree
* **Evergreen/fast**
* **Woody capsules**
* **Ht: 8-10m/20-30ft**

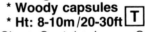

Since Captain James Cook brewed a beverage from tiny leaves of a New Zealand **Leptospermum,** the genus has been blessed with the name Tea Tree, though nobody these days seems eager to repeat the experiment.

The really useful species is **L. laevigatum,** the Coastal Tea Tree, found from Tasmania well up into Queensland. It is salt-resistant and of tremendous value both as a windbreak in coastal gardens and for stabilizing drifting sands.

The Coastal Tea Tree grows to 10m, but is more often seen in a variety of contorted shapes, sometimes quite horizontal from its exposure to gales. The bark is stringy, grey and picturesque, the foliage fine and dense.

Liquidambar styraciflua
leaf detail

LIQUIDAMBAR

Sweetgum
* **Deciduous/fast** C
* **Autumn colour**
* **Ht: to 40m/120ft** T H

The mellifluous name **Liquidambar styraciflua** has been given to one of the great specimen trees of the world, the North American Sweetgum. Native to a large belt from Texas to lower New York State, and right through the Smoky Mountains, it is strangely disappointing in its native haunts, looking somewhat gaunt and crushed as it struggles for survival among more pushy, widely spreading trees. But get it out on its own in a lawn with access to a good supply of water and up it shoots, straight as a die for 25 or even 40 metres, an elongated pyramid up to 15m in diameter at ground level. The grey bark is deeply furrowed, hanging in cork-like flaps from almost every branch. The greenish flowers appear in small clusters at the ends of twigs, developing as they are fertilized into globular burr-like fruit.

But the foliage is **Liquidambar's** special glory. The leaves are rather star-shaped with five or seven serrated lobes. They are bright green, turning an incredible range of colours

83

LIQUIDAMBAR (continued)

in autumn. One tree may become palest gold and pink, another purple, so dark it is almost black; still others scarlet, gold and orange. Good varieties are propagated true to colour only from root-cuttings of an individual tree.

Liquidambars are greedy feeders. Nothing will grow around them and they'll even send marauding roots up into nearby pots in search of water. Their timber is used in many types of furniture and for decorative inlays and veneers.

Far away in southern China and Taiwan, its only close relative, the Chinese Sweetgum, **L. formosana,** is of similar appearance in all respects but two — the leaves are three-lobed only, and the bark does not hang in decorative folds. It is altogether an inferior tree, though very useful in its native land.

Liquidambars are quite frost-resistant when mature, but equally suited to warm coastal climates so long as they are not in range of flying salt spray.

The name **Liquidambar** is not an allusion to the tree's autumn colour, but to a resin prepared from the Chinese species.

Liquidambar styraciflua
Sweet Gum

Liquidambar formosana
Chinese Sweet Gum

84

LIRIODENDRON

Tulip Tree, Tulip Poplar
* **Deciduous /fast**
* **Autumn colour**
* **Ht: to 25m /80ft** C T

Closely related to the **Magnolias,** the Tulip Tree, **Liriodendron tulipifera,** is native to the entire eastern seaboard of the United States except for the northern New England states and southern Florida. A fast grower, but slow to flower, it may reach a respectable 7m in as many years, and ultimately the arrow-straight trunk may top 25m. In its cool native forests it has been measured to twice that height!

The deciduous leaves are unique: long-stemmed and four-lobed, with the appearance of having been lopped off at the apex, they unfurl quite late in spring, well after the Maples, and turn to a blaze of molten gold in autumn, dropping quite early to leave the tree a stark, angular framework of bare trunk and branches.

The name Tulip Tree is in reference to the handsome flowers, which are indeed like Tulips. They are coloured a rich lime-green with orange centres, and appear well after the foliage, often at too great a height to pick. After the petals drop, a cone-shaped seed cluster is revealed, which persists until the branches are bare in winter; then the casing falls apart and the seeds float away on a single wing.

There are exquisite varieties with the leaves beautifully margined in yellow, although the lighter areas tend to darken in late summer.

The botanical name, **Liriodendron tulipifera,** means tulip-bearing lily tree. The timber is a useful, close-grained hardwood — if you could bear to cut it down — and is known in the trade as Tulip Poplar.

Right around the world, in central China, the only other species is found, but not often seen in cultivation.

This is **L. chinense,** a much smaller tree rarely reaching 17m, really a far better proposition for the home garden. Its leaves are slightly larger than the American species, though also four-lobed. The flowers are dull green and yellow.

Liriodendron tulipifera
Tulip tree

Liriodendron CV 'Aureo-Marginatum'
Variegated Tulip Tree

Litchi sinensis
Lychee

LITCHI

Lychee
* **Evergreen /slow** [T]
* **Summer fruit**
* **Ht: to 15m /50ft** [H]

Surely 800 million Chinese can't be wrong when they select the Lychee as their favourite fruit? My personal idea of heaven includes a basket of these delectable morsels, fresh from the tree and lightly chilled on a summer's day.

The tree they come from is native to southern China, India and the Philippines and is known botanically as **Litchi sinensis,** from its old Chinese name. It is a graceful tree, generally slim-trunked and growing as tall as 15m in a cool, deep soil with plenty of moisture. Though tropical in origin, it is able to stand a few degrees of frost when well established, and may start to bear as early as five years from seed. But the seed must be sown within a few days of picking, or it is no longer viable. Trees are raised commercially by air-layering or inarched grafting of superior varieties.

Litchi sinensis
fruit detail

The spreading crown consists of evergreen compound leaves, each made up of two to four pairs of drooping, pointed leaflets. These are palest green, gold or even pink when young. The tiny yellowish flowers are borne in terminal panicles. The 4cm oval fruit appear in dangling clusters, green at first, then deep red and finally brown at maturity. Each has a thin, warty shell surrounding a mass of delicately fragrant pulp rather the texture of a grape. This contains one large seed.

Lychees can be eaten fresh or dried, when they look and taste something like an oversized raisin. Huge quantities of them are canned and exported from South-East Asia every summer.

MACADAMIA

Queensland Nut,
Hawaiian Nut
* **Evergreen /fast** [T]
* **Summer nuts**
* **Ht: 5-20m /15-60ft** [H]

Carrying coals to Newcastle is nothing com-

Macadamia integrifolia
fruit detail

Macadamia tetraphylla
foliage detail

MACADAMIA (continued)

pared to the way Australian tourists pour back from Hawaii clutching all sorts of containers of the delicious 'Hawaiian Nuts' they've been sold. The nuts grow on a tree called **Macadamia integrifolia** and it comes from Queensland, Australia, whence it was first taken to Hawaii in 1890.

Three species of **Macadamia** are grown, all of them handsome, evergreen trees for the subtropical and temperate garden. **M. integrifolia** grows to 20m tall, but not quite as wide, and has relatively smooth-edged adult leaves. **M. tetraphylla** is not so tall, but is wider in the spread of its branches, and its leaves are finely serrated and wavy. **M. ternifolia** is the runt of the genus, a mere 5m, with pink young foliage, and the adult leaves coarsely serrated; its nuts are smaller than the others, somewhat bitter and inedible. All three bear long, hanging racemes of tiny flowers, **M. integrifolia's** being white, the others pink.

The nuts ripen in late summer in a temperate climate, but the trees flower and fruit continuously in the tropics.

They are named for Dr John Macadam, an Australian medical practitioner.

Maclura pomifera
Osage Orange

Magnolia grandiflora
Bull Bay

MACLURA

Osage Orange
* **Deciduous /slow**
* **Autumn fruits**
* **Ht: 20m /60ft**

Whoever originated the popular name of this extraordinary North American tree must have been somewhat mixed-up. Orange indeed! The fruits don't resemble citrus in size, shape or colour, and certainly not in flavour. But believe it or not **Maclura** is actually most closely related to the tropical breadfruit (see **Artocarpus**).

Native to the southern central United States, **Maclura pomifera** has become naturalized all over that nation, and is occasionally found in old country gardens of Australia. It will grow in particularly impoverished soil, and in drier parts of Europe it is sometimes seen pruned as a spiny, tallish hedge-plant.

The large, irregularly-shaped fruits are of curiosity value only. They are quite inedible and are about the size of a grapefruit.

MAGNOLIA

Bull Bay
* **Evergreen /fast**
* **Summer flowers**
* **Ht: to 25m /80ft**

Through a tremendous range of climates from cold temperate to subtropical, the ultimate ornamental tree is a **Magnolia** of one sort or another. This is thanks to the fact that the genus has two homelands — the cold far west of China and southern USA on the warm gulf of Mexico.

The Chinese species are deciduous, the American species are among the most handsome of evergreens.

The most commonly seen is undoubtedly the giant Bull Bay or Southern Magnolia, **M. grandiflora,** which may reach 25m where the winters are warm enough. Its large simple leaves look as if they have been lacquered on top and sprayed with brown flock beneath. These are often preserved with paraffin as winter decoration, long after the summer flowers have faded.

MALUS

Apple, Crabapple
* **Deciduous /fast** $\boxed{C}$
* **Autumn fruits**
* **5-15m /15-45ft** $\boxed{T}$

If the cost of medical insurance continues to rise it may pay us to remember the old saying 'an apple a day keeps the doctor away' and plant an apple tree in our own gardens.

From the vast number of Apples and Crabapples listed it is hard to believe that they are all varieties of only twenty-five species.

This includes over a thousand named varieties of the eating apple, **Malus domestica,** varying from 2.5 to 10cm in diameter, and tinted every possible combination of green, yellow, red and pink.

Apples are all native to the temperate zone of the Northern Hemisphere, though they are now grown in cooler climates everywhere. They are deciduous members of the rose family, a fact which isn't surprising if you look closely at their flowers and leaves.

The original European Crab, **M. sylvestris,** has white flowers and is rather thorny. Its 2.5cm fruit are green, sour and sometimes red tinted. They make a delicious, tart jelly.

The Japanese Crab, **M. floribunda,** is a graceful, heavily flowering tree that scarcely reaches 8m, ideal for the average garden. Its tiny 5mm fruit may be red or yellow.

The Prairie Crab, **M. ioensis,** is an American species, 10m in the wild, but often quite dwarfed in cultivation. It has hairy, often lobed leaves, semi-double pink blossom, rather sparse yellow and green fruit.

M. hupehensis is from China and grows to 8m. The leaves are long and slender, the single flowers white, the charming red fruit on long stems are quite miniature.

M. X purpurea 'Eleyi' is the Purple Crab, a decorative small tree with bronzy leaves and flowers of deep purple-pink. The fruit, too, are coloured a purplish red.

Other species grown for the decorative effect of their fruits include the cultivars 'Gorgeous' with vivid scarlet crabs, and 'Golden Hornet' in which the fruits are orange-yellow.

Malus, the botanical name of both Apples and Crabs, is the original Roman name of the wild European species.

Malus domestica
Apple

Malus X 'Gravenstein'
Gravenstein Apple

Malus X 'Gorgeous'
Hybrid Crab

Malus X *hupehensis*
Chinese Crab

Malus X 'Golden Gem'
Hybrid Crab

MANGIFERA

Mango
* **Evergreen /fast**
* **Spring-autumn fruits**
* **Ht: to 30m /100ft**

[T]
[H]

Sometimes known as the Peach of the Tropics, **Mangifera indica** is hailed in its native India as King of Fruits and is the subject of many legends. A handsome, tropical tree, preferring a warm, dry winter to produce well, the Mango may reach 30m in South-East Asia and the Philippines, but rarely half that in warm temperate to subtropical climates. In both areas, however, its spread may be very wide.

The leaves are narrow, leathery and up to 33cm long. Dark green and stiff when mature, they are often brightly pink and hanging as new foliage, having a distinct odour of turpentine when crushed.

In mid-winter, the Mango tree is very picturesque, as curved, upright-pointing panicles of tiny pink flowers appear at every branch tip. These are followed by the great 15cm fruit that soon pull the stems down under their weight. In tropical areas these continue to ripen from spring right through to autumn, according to variety. And there are many varieties in many shapes and colours: yellow, orange, red, green, pink and purple; banana-shaped, orange-shaped, oval or kidney-shaped.

Improved varieties must be propagated from cuttings, but do not bear so well as ordinary seedlings. Consequently the fruit seen most commonly on the market is from the more commercially practical seedling trees, and often fibrous. Superior named varieties are quite free of fibre.

The botanical name is an extraordinary hybrid of Latin and Hindustani! *Mango* being the original Indian name and *fero* meaning to bear in Latin.

Mangifera indica
Mango

Mango, fruit detail

MANILKARA

Sapodilla, Chicle Tree
* **Evergreen /fast**
* **Summer fruit**
* **Ht: to 35m /120ft** H

This tall, handsome tree from Central America is so decorative, its hidden talents come as a surprise.

The leaves of **Manilkara zapota** are dark glossy green; the single, white flowers are followed by furry fruits the size of tennis balls. These are full of a yellowish pulp with tiny black seeds, something like a Kiwi fruit, and equally delicious. Known as Sapodillas, they are favourite dessert fruits in tropical America. The sap, known as chicle, after much refining and flavouring, becomes the chewing gum so many of us enjoy.

Manilkara can be propagated from seed, but grafted seedlings grow quicker.

Manilkara zapota
Sapodilla

Maytenus boaria
Mayten Tree

MAYTENUS

Mayten Tree
* **Deciduous /slow**
* **Summer foliage**
* **Ht: to 8m /25ft** C T

A beautiful Chilean tree with all the grace of a weeping willow (and few of its disadvantages), **Maytenus boaria** is less widely seen away from the Americas than its many virtues deserve. It has the same weeping branches with slender, pale-green leaves — but they are evergreen and lightly serrated. Its roots are not invasive, so it can be planted close to your house and makes a decorative patio tree either in the ground or in a large tub. It also makes the perfect background tree for an oriental-type garden setting. It is not small, may ultimately reach 16m in height in an ideal moist but well-drained position. But in normal garden conditions it is unlikely to reach 6m in height and about the same in width in much under 12 years. Greenish flowers are inconspicuous, are followed by tiny red berries. Superior varieties are propagated from cuttings.

MELALEUCA

Paperbark, Cajeput Tree
* **Evergreen /fast**
* **Decorative bark**
* **Ht: 7-25m /21-75ft** [T] [H]

One of the best-loved Australian genera world-wide, the decorative **Melaleucas** now flourish in every subtropical to temperate area of the world, often where other trees kick up their heels. There are over a hundred species, known mostly for their decorative peeling barks and pollen-rich flower spikes on which hundreds of long-stamened flowers are arranged in the form of a bottlebrush, generally white or cream in all of the tree-sized species.

Most common is the ubiquitous **M. quin-quenervia,** known as the Broadleaf Paperbark or Cajeput tree. A handsome, spreading giant growing to 25m high when planted on its own in damp ground, it is more often seen crowded in brackish swamps as a collection of slim, white-trunked saplings, with all the character of a field of clothes props. In this guise it has become unpopular in the state of Florida, where it may well succeed in taking over the famous Everglades.

In contrast, the Hong Kong Government plants it widely to help stabilize swampy farming areas of the New Territories. Like it or loathe it, everyone agrees it is the most reliable of trees for damp ground.

A second worthwhile species is the decorative Snow in Summer, **M. linarifolia,** which never outgrows its welcome. Rarely above 7m, it has a spreading habit, inclining towards multiple trunks.

In the Bracelet Honeymyrtle, **M. armillaris,** the leaves are modified to needleform, and the bark more furrowed than flaking. The dense flower-spikes are almost pure white and about 7.5cm long; **M. armillaris** may grow to 10m and is particularly dense-foliaged. It is often seen group-planted as a windbreak in exposed positions.

Melaleucas are propagated from cuttings, and the botanical name is a combination of the Greek words for black and white. This presumably refers to the extreme tonal contrast between dark and light sections of the tree.

Melaleuca quinquenervia ▶
Cajeput Tree

Melia azederach
Chinaberry

Mespilus germanica
Medlar

MELIA

Syrian Bead Tree,
Chinaberry
* **Deciduous/fast**
* **Autumn berries**
* **Ht: to 20m/60ft**

C T H

Today there is hardly a country on earth where **Melia azederach** is not grown for its useful and decorative qualities.

In tropical climates it shoots up to 20m and more, with a spreading crown that provides useful shade for most of the year. In Texas, Australia and Persia it grows usually wider than its height.

In all areas it bears handsome leaves (like those of the European **Fraxinus**) that turn bright yellow in autumn.

Lilac spring flower clusters are followed by a mass of berries, green at first but turning orange as the summer warms up. They persist long after leaf fall, giving the bare tree a most attractive appearance.

Melia is easy to propagate from seed or cuttings.

MESPILUS

Medlar
* **Deciduous/slow**
* **Autumn fruit/colour**
* **Ht: to 7m/20ft**

C T

Outside Europe the Medlar is probably the least commonly grown fruit tree of the Rose family (Apples, Pears and Quinces are others), and hasn't been very much in demand since refrigeration and canning made a year-round fruit supply possible.

But in earlier times it was valued as the last fruit to hold on the tree. It was not even regarded as fit to eat until it was frost-bitten and half rotten!

Mespilus germanica is the botanical name of the curious twisted tree it grows on, and unlike others of the Rose family its leaves turn a rich, rusty brown in autumn. The fruit is a little larger than a golf ball, and has a fuzzy brown surface and five seeds.

From these seeds the Medlars are propagated, although a better method is to graft them on Quince or Hawthorn stock.

METASEQUOIA

Dawn Redwood
* **Deciduous /fast**
* **Autumn colour**
* **Ht: to 35m /120ft**

[C]

[T]

From a Western point-of-view probably the newest tree in cultivation, the lovely deciduous conifer **Metasequoia glyptostroboides** was discovered as recently as 1941 in China's Sichuan province.

An overnight sensation as a new relative of Florida's Swamp Cypresses (**Taxodium,** which see) and California's **Sequoias,** it was rushed into cultivation, seed being distributed worldwide in 1948.

In nature, the Dawn Redwood grows to 35m and has already reached 8m in cultivation. It is a light and airy conical tree with palest-green feathery foliage. This turns pink and amber before dropping in the autumn.

Metasequoia glyptostroboides
Dawn Redwood

MORINDA

Indian Mulberry, Noni
* **Evergreen /fast**
* **Warm weather fruit**
* **Ht: to 7m /20ft**

[H]

A small tree with brilliantly shining foliage, the Indian Mulberry, **Morinda,** is found naturally in South-East Asia, Australia and the Pacific Islands.

Morinda citrifolia is popular in subtropical gardens for the decorative, shiny foliage and many-flowered heads of white blossom which develop into a curious, compound fruit, rather like a small Breadfruit or large Mulberry.

The ancient Polynesians (who called it Noni), extracted dyes of several colours from parts of the plant. They even ate the fruit in hard times, for they are edible if rather unpalatable.

The botanical name **Morinda** is merely a contraction from the Latin *morus* meaning mulberry, and *indica* meaning Indian. However, it is actually related to the **Gardenia** rather than the Mulberry.

Morinda citrifolia
Indian Mulberry

Morus rubra
Red Mulberry

MORUS

Mulberry
* **Deciduous/slow**
* **Late spring fruits**
* **Ht: 10-25m/30-75ft** C T

'With patience, the mulberry leaf becomes a silken robe,' says an old Chinese proverb, and that about sums up the most important quality of the **Morus** or Mulberries, a deciduous genus principally found in the Americas and Asia.

All **Morus** species are cultivated as food for silkworms, and the species **M. alba,** the White Mulberry, is preferred for the purpose because it grows faster, up to 25m in China, and thus produces more, though smaller, leaves. These are sometimes three-lobed, and a decorative weeping variety **M. alba pendula** is much favoured as a garden specimen.

Morus nigra, the Black Mulberry, is a fruit of a different colour! Native to Persia and nearby areas, it is a slow grower with nobbly bark, and often develops a wide-spreading, picturesque shape without any help from the gardener. Rarely above 10m in height, its large, rough-textured, coarsely-toothed leaves are somewhat heart-shaped and all of 20cm long.

The drooping flower catkins are uninteresting, but are followed in late spring by incredibly juicy, acid-sweet fruits that resemble blackberries. These are red at first, ripening to almost black, and several named varieties, with larger, juicier fruit are available. Eat them raw or cooked, make them into jams or pies or crush them to enjoy the juice with your favourite drink.

A third species, **M. rubra,** the Red Mulberry, is native to North America and rarely grown elsewhere because its fruits are inferior. It grows to 20m, and often develops a particularly grotesque, attractive shape.

All Mulberry fruits stain faces, hands and everything in sight, but the stains can be removed with the juice of a green mulberry.

Morus is the ancient Latin name of the genus, which has many named varieties, differing both in habit and in leaf-shape.

Mulberries can be propagated from very large cuttings, even whole branches.

Morus nigra
Black Mulberry

Nephelium lappaceum
Rambutan

NEPHELIUM

Rambutan, Pulasan
* **Evergreen /fast**
* **Autumn fruit**
* **Ht: to 15m /45ft** H

Found in many parts of tropical South-East Asia, and even in the north of Australia, the genus **Nephelium** includes about seventy species, many of them valued locally for their fruits.

They are closely related to both the Lychee and Loong Ngan (see **Litchi** and **Euphoria**), but only the following two species are grown much away from their native areas.

The Pulasan **(N. mutabile),** a Javanese tree of some 15m with compound evergreen leaves and rather nobbly red fruit resembling the Lychee.

The Rambutan **(N. lappaceum)** is seen universally in tropical gardens. It grows to roughly the same size, has leathery, bay-like leaves and in late summer bears masses of 5cm fruits covered with soft spines. These are filled with delicious translucent pulp.

Canned rambutans are served in many Malaysian and Chinese restaurants, but the tree is easy to grow from seed if the climate is warm.

The botanical name **Nephelium** is from the Greek, meaning little cloud, presumably in reference to the masses of small, whitish summer flowers.

Nothofagus moorei
Negrohead Beech

Nothofagus obliqua
Roble Beech

NOTHOFAGUS

Southern Beech,
False Beech
* **Evergreen/slow**
* **Handsome foliage**
* **Ht: 25-70m/75-220ft**

The handsome Beech trees of the Northern Hemisphere (see **Fagus**), have a similar looking group of close relatives in the Southern Hemisphere. They are named **Nothofagus,** meaning False Beeches, and like many other southern genera are scattered about Australia, New Zealand and South America, pointing to a common origin, perhaps in prehistoric Antarctica.

There are at least twenty-five species growing in the southern half of the globe in climatic areas varying from cold temperate to almost tropical, so one or more of them can be grown anywhere, though the South American species are more cold-resistant.

The Southern Beeches are most variable in habit, ranging from dwarf, almost scrubby plants in windy Tierra del Fuego to giant timber trees in the forests of Australia and New Zealand. The Tasmanian species **N. cunninghamii** has been recorded up to 70m in height. Known as the Myrtle Beech, it is an important timber tree, bears dark, triangularly toothed leaves in fan-shaped sprays.

The foliage of Southern Beeches is much like that of their northern cousins, though more usually evergreen. The seeds (or beech nuts) are also very much alike.

Among other more popular types are the deciduous Chilean **N. antarctica,** which may reach 30m and has leaves less than 2.5cm in length, the evergreen **N. dombeyi** from Chile and Argentina, which has glossy, evergreen leaves about the same size; New Zealand's evergreen **N. fusca** or Red Beech has slightly larger leaves and is a faster-growing tree. **N. moorei,** the Negrohead Beech, is an Australian species, reaching 50m. Fast growing, broad-headed, with a dense foliage cover, it is not frost-hardy. The pointed oval leaves are evergreen and may reach 7.5cm in length; they have a bronzy lustre. **N. obliqua,** the Roble Beech from Chile, is most adaptable to colder gardens. It may reach 30m and the large leaves are deeply toothed. A valuable timber tree.

Nyssa sylvatica
fruit and foliage

Nyssa sylvatica
Tupelo

NYSSA

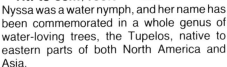

Tupelo, Black Gum
* **Deciduous/fast**
* **Autumn colour/fruit**
* **Ht: to 35m/100ft**

Nyssa was a water nymph, and her name has been commemorated in a whole genus of water-loving trees, the Tupelos, native to eastern parts of both North America and Asia.

The commonly cultivated species is the deciduous **Nyssa sylvatica,** an ideal and decorative specimen tree for damp or ill-drained positions. Of a vertical, pyramidal habit, it may grow to 20m in a really moist waterside position, and have a branch spread of 5m — though generally less.

The 10cm leaves are shiny, smooth-margined and slightly wider towards the tip than the base. In autumn they turn to wondrous fiery red, reflecting superbly in nearby water. The uninteresting greenish flowers appear on long stems originating in the leaf axils, and are succeeded by brilliant deep-blue fruits, about 1 cm long, and a stunning colour contrast to the autumn foliage. The bark is a rich brownish grey, usually broken up into tile-like slabs on older trees.

Another member of the genus is **Nyssa aquatica,** the Water Tupelo from southern USA. This is a similar tree, but usually grows right in swamps or shallow water, developing a buttressed trunk. The oval fruits may reach 2.5cm in diameter, and the leaves are sometimes slightly toothed. It is an important timber tree, with flowers most attractive to bees, and producing delicious honey.

OLEA

Olive
* **Evergreen** /fast  C
* **Summer fruits** T
* **Ht: to 8m /25ft**

In Western civilization at least, the Olive is undoubtedly the oldest tree in continuous cultivation.

Its botanical name **Olea** is the ancient Roman word for oil; and in modern times, when we think of olive oil merely as an ingredient of salad dressing or soap, it is difficult to imagine its importance to the ancient world. It was the basis of cosmetics; it was their only method of lubrication; it provided precious lighting at night, and a valuable foodstuff by day.

The Common Olive, **Olea europaea,** is not a large tree, rarely exceeding 8m, but it can become enormously gnarled and thick with age, living to 1,500 years and more. Its slender leaves are silver-backed, its flowers tiny and yellowish, and the oil-rich fruits are up to 4cm in diameter, glossy black when ripe.

More commonly seen away from the Mediterranean is the similar **Olea africana,** found naturally over a wide area from Africa to China. Its leaves are slightly larger, often backed with gold rather than silver. The round fruits rarely exceed 1cm in diameter. They too contain oil, but the tree is rarely cultivated for this purpose. It is often seen as a street tree, being extremely well suited to dry pavement conditions.

Olea africana
fruit detail

Olea africana
African Olive

100

ONCOBA

(No popular name)
* **Evergreen/slow** [T]
* **Summer fruits** [H]
* **Ht: to 6m/20ft**

A smallish, spiny tree from tropical Africa, **Oncoba spinosa** has few relations in cultivation beyond the **Idesia** (which see) and the exotic **Hydnocarpus,** source of precious Chaulmoogra oil, used in the treatment of leprosy. It is however seen in many botanic garden collections, and is greatly valued in the tropics for almost all its parts.

The shining, serrated 10cm leaves are used for medicinal purposes; the 7.5cm white flowers (so like **Camellias**) are picked for their fragrance; they are followed by beautiful golden 6cm fruits which are full of a tangy, edible pulp that tastes rather like a pomegranate. There is also a thriving cottage industry fashioning the dried fruit husks into small containers for snuff and other stimulants. If you can procure a plant, it makes a decorative addition to the warm-temperate garden. Plant in a sheltered position.

Oncoba spinosa
fruit detail

OSTRYA

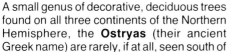

Hop Hornbeam,
Leverwood
* **Deciduous/fast** [C]
* **Autumn colour** [T]
* **Ht: to 20m/65ft**

A small genus of decorative, deciduous trees found on all three continents of the Northern Hemisphere, the **Ostryas** (their ancient Greek name) are rarely, if at all, seen south of the Equator.

But in the cooler climates they love, they'll easily reach 20m in height, and are particularly cultivated for their show of autumn colour. The popular name is Hop Hornbeam, which describes them perfectly. The handsome toothed leaves resemble those of the Hornbeam **(Carpinus),** while the hanging fruit clusters resemble those of the edible Hop **(Humulus,** used in the brewing of beer).

European **O. carpinifolia** is most commonly seen, while American gardens are home to **O. virginiana,** sometimes known as Ironwood. It has dark brown bark, large fruit.

Ostrya carpinifolia
Hop Hornbeam

PANDANUS

Screw Pine
* **Evergreen/fast** [T]
* **Summer fruits**
* **Ht: to 7m/20ft** [H]

Popularly known as either Screw Pines or Walking Palms, there are several hundred species of **Pandanus,** found naturally from Malagasy to the Pacific Islands, and commonly seen right on the water's edge.

They are a decorative asset in seaside gardens of warm climates, grown for their profuse fountains of spirally arranged, razor-edged leaves. The branched spikes of tiny white flowers are followed by fruit-heads about 20cm in diameter, and with the appearance of a pineapple.

Commonly seen **P. odoratissimus** reaches 8m and may spread even wider, the stiff branches supporting themselves on stilt-like masses of aerial roots.

P. veitchii rarely passes 5m, but its magnificent variegated foliage has made it more popular in cultivation. Young specimens make elegant indoor plants.

All **Pandanus** are propagated from suckers, or from the tough seeds, which must be soaked for twenty-four hours before planting.

Pandanus veitchii
Screw Pine

Pandanus odoratissimus
fruit detail

Parrotia persica
Persian Witchhazel

PARROTIA

Persian Witchhazel
* **Deciduous/fast** [C]
* **Autumn colour**
* **Ht: to 7m/22ft** [T]

Untidily shaped in cultivation and tending more to the habit of a large shrub than my idea of a tree, the Persian Witchhazel, or **Parrotia,** makes a splendid autumn feature in a good year, but needs a sheltered position.

In its native Persian mountains, it is said to grow tall and straight with a broad crown, but all the garden specimens I have seen have favoured much shorter multiple trunks and low, often weeping, branches. The deciduous leaves are splendid at almost any time of year, oval and blunt-ended with rather rippled

PARROTIA (continued)

edges and a distinctly quilted effect on the upper surface. They unfold in the earliest spring, just after the flowers, which are rather uninteresting clusters of blood-red stamens that pop out of a pair of woolly brown bracts.

P. persica was named after the German naturalist F.W. Parrot, and is a particularly useful tree in alkaline soils. It is easily propagated from seed, layers or cuttings, and has no particular use beyond its decorative qualities.

Persea americana
Avocado, fruit

Persea americana
Avocado Tree

PERSEA

Avocado, Alligator Pear
* **Evergreen/fast**
* **Fruits all year**
* **Ht: to 20m/60ft**

The delicious avocadoes of which so many of us are fond ripen on **Persea americana,** a handsome 15m tree with glossy foliage. Evergreen in tropical areas, semi-deciduous elsewhere, it demands good drainage.

It is claimed that some four hundred named varieties of Avocado are in cultivation; all are variants of the original species, which is naturally scattered about Central America and the West Indies. To the home fancier, any one would be a treasure, whether its fruit was round, oval or pear-shaped, and whether the skin was green, purple or black at the time of ripening.

All types of fruit contain the same sumptuous lime-green pulp, rich in oils and iodine.

Those of us in cooler temperate climates must be content with summer-ripening varieties. But as one goes further towards the tropics, there are varieties that ripen in any season of the year.

As the average home Avocado tree requires at least seven years to fruit, the best advice is to buy only a guaranteed bisexual graft from your nursery.

Avocadoes bear fuzzy yellowish bisexual flowers at branch tips (sometimes only in alternate years), and many trees lose much foliage at this time.

Phyllanthus acidus
Otaheite Gooseberry

Phytolacca dioica
Bella Sombra

PHYLLANTHUS

Otaheite Gooseberry,
Myrobalan
* **Deciduous /fast**
* **Summer fruits**
* **Ht: 10m /30ft** [H]

Phyllanthus are represented in warm-climate gardens by two small trees grown for their edible fruits. These are **P. acidus,** the Otaheite Gooseberry, and **P. emblica,** the Myrobalan, from South-East Asia. Both trees reach 10m and are deciduous, with single stalkless leaves arranged in a flat plane along each twig.

The late-summer fruits of **P. acidus** are ribbed and bright yellow, clustering around the trunk and branches; those of **P. emblica** are pale green and smooth. Both may be enjoyed stewed with sugar, or made into jams and pickles.

The two **Phyllanthus** species are propagated from seeds or green cuttings.

PHYTOLACCA

Ombu, Bella Sombra
* **Evergreen /fast** [T]
* **Shade tree**
* **Ht: to 16m /50ft** [H]

The strange and wonderful **Phytolacca dioica** from Central and South America can in time become a real conversation piece in the large temperate to tropical garden. Just see the root development in the specimen I photographed in southern California! This enormous growth is designed to protect the otherwise shallow-rooted tree from storm and drought in its native pampas environment, and the wide-spreading branches of evergreen foliage have led to its cultivation in many warm climates as a shade tree (in Spanish, *bella sombra* means sweet shade). Beware of spending too much time lazing under it in dry weather though, for the timber, like that of many fast-growing trees, is light, spongy and brittle. Whole branches may snap and drop off! The leaves are smooth and oval, small white flowers are borne in racemes at branch tips. The multiple red berry fruits that follow are mildly poisonous.

Picea glauca
White Spruce

Picea CV 'Kosteriana'
Colorado Blue Spruce

PICEA

Spruce
* **Evergreen /fast**
* **Decorative cones**
* **Ht: 3-70m /9-220ft**

[C]

[T]

If the genus **Picea** contained only one tree, and that was the wonderful Colorado Blue Spruce (**P. pungens** 'Kosteriana'), it would still be listed among the most important tree groups in the world.

But there are between thirty and fifty species and at least four times as many beautiful cultivars from which to make a choice. All of them are native to a high-altitude, cooler-climate zone running from

Picea abies
Norway Spruce

Picea abies
cone detail

PICEA (continued)

Europe through Asia Minor, northward to Siberia and Japan, and right across North America.

In nature, the trees are generally of a tall pyramidal habit with stiff upward-pointing branches that droop only with the weight of age. They are often confused with the Firs (**Abies**) but vary in several important minor details. First, the leaves, which are spirally arranged, leave peg-like bases on the twig when they fall. Second, their mature cones always hang downwards.

Spruces are far more tolerant of pollution and climatic variation than the Firs, but do not transplant well and should be started out as young as possible. Moist, acid soil is preferred, but many of them can cope with a degree of lime.

There are three giant species in the genus: **P. abies,** the Norway Spruce of north and central Europe; **P. sitchensis,** the Sitka Spruce of north-east America; and **P.**

spinulosa, the Sikkim Spruce of the Himalayas. Any of these may commonly reach 70m in their native forests, and they are regarded as valuable timber trees.

Spruces with weeping branches include: **P. breweriana,** Brewer's Weeping Spruce from California; **P. omorika pendula,** the Serbian Spruce from Yugoslavia; and the hybrid **P. standishii** with blue foliage. All grow to around 30m.

The North American White Spruce, **P. glauca,** is grown commercially for pulping into newsprint, but its dwarf cultivar **P.g.** 'Albertiana Conica' is one of the most popular small specimen trees for landscaping in the cooler climate, rarely exceeding 3m.

P. orientalis from the Caucasus and **P. jezoensis** from Japan are popular specimen trees, neither topping 35m. But most widely grown for this purpose is the Colorado Spruce, **P. pungens,** generally in one of its blue-leafed forms such as the CVs 'Argentea', 'Glauca', 'Kosteriana' and 'Moerheimii'.

All Spruce species are fragrant with resin.

PIMENTA

Allspice, Bay Rum Tree
* **Evergreen/fast**
* **Summer berries**
* **Ht: 10-13m/30-40ft** H

'Take me to Jamaica where the rum cums frum' ran a once-popular song, and the words might have applied equally to the Bay Rum Tree, one of a small genus of West Indian trees grown for their aromatic parts.

Called **Pimenta** botanically, they are closely related to the Australian Eucalypts and Lillypillies.

Pimenta acris, the Bayberry or Wild Clove, is a 10m evergreen, with pea-sized berries that are used in cooking.

More highly valued are ripened, dark-brown berries of **P. dioica,** ground to make allspice, a popular culinary additive.

P. racemosa, the Bay Rum Tree, is the source of Oil of Bay, which is extracted both from leaves and twigs.

All species are propagated from half-ripened cuttings, and grow best in gardens of hot climates.

Pimenta dioica
Allspice

Pinus radiata
Monterey Pine

PINUS

Pine
* **Evergreen/fast** C
* **Ornamental cones**
* **Ht: 15-70m/45-225ft** T

Most widespread and instantly recognizable of the conifers, the Pines have lent their old Roman name not only to a genus, **Pinus,** but to the entire botanical family Pinaceae that includes the other principal coniferous genera of the Northern Hemisphere as well (**Abies, Cedrus, Larix, Picea** and many other groups).

There are actually only about eighty species of Pine, all native to the northern continents, but their climatic range stretches from beyond the Arctic Circle to subtropical regions near the Equator. Some are mountain trees; some actually flourish in almost pure sand by the seashore. But the vast majority will grow in conditions which any sensible tree would reject out of hand, clinging like grim death to rocky hillsides, hanging

Pinus ponderosa
Western Yellow Pine

PINUS (continued)

over gorges or sprouting on windy promontories stretching way out into the ocean.

Several species including the European **P. pinaster** and the American **P. radiata** have been naturalized in the Southern Hemisphere where they grow better than in their own home areas.

Pines, as mentioned previously, are instantly recognizable, if only by their leaves, which have evolved into a needle-shape, often perfectly rounded and appearing in bunches of two, three or five according to species, each bundle wrapped at its base in a sheath-like membrane. The needles may be less than 2.5cm long as in the Japanese **P. parviflora,** or up to 45cm long as in the American **P. palustris.**

The young growth of Pines is in the form of a vertical spike known as a 'candle'. Growth of small trees can be directed or modified by twisting these candles right off. Male Pine flowers appear in a ring of small, cylindrical, upright catkins around the new growth. They vary from red to yellow in colour, and scatter pollen abundantly in early summer in an effort to fertilize the female flowers elsewhere on the same tree.

Pinus pinaster
Maritime Pine

Pinus peuce
Macedonian Pine

PINUS (continued)

Fertilized female flowers develop into cones, which may be borne singly or in clusters, again according to species. These take two years to ripen, after which their overlapping scales open to discharge the seeds in early autumn.

Cones differ widely, and are a principal key to the identification of Pine species. They may be small and egg-shaped, or long and cylindrical, with any number of variations in-between. Some of them are nearly 60cm in length and release their seeds while still on the tree, others fall before opening.

There is a Pine for almost every type of soil, and the selection of the right one is an important branch of forestry. The timber of most species is both soft and fragrant, and of great importance in the building and paper industries. The trees are also the source of important oils and resins and are highly flammable.

The general habit of most European and North American Pines is conical when young, but with a development of high, spreading branches on older trees. Exceptions are several alpine species.

Several of the Japanese Pines are quite different, twisting their branches and trunks in a naturally picturesque fashion which has done much to inspire the art of bonsai tree training.

Pinus densiflora
Japanese Red Pine

Pinus thunbergii
Japanese Black Pine

Pisonia alba
Lettuce Tree

Pistacia vera
Pistachio

Pistacia chinensis
Chinese Pistachio

PISONIA

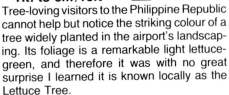

Lettuce Tree
* **Deciduous/fast**
* **Decorative foliage**
* **Ht: to 5m/15ft** H

Tree-loving visitors to the Philippine Republic cannot help but notice the striking colour of a tree widely planted in the airport's landscaping. Its foliage is a remarkable light lettuce-green, and therefore it was with no great surprise I learned it is known locally as the Lettuce Tree.

Native to Malaysia and the southern Philippine area, its botanical name is **Pisonia alba,** and it is closely related to the Bougain-villeas. Not a large tree, rarely reaching 5m, its leaves are deciduous, slightly furry and shaped like an elongated heart. Though the timber is spongy and useless, the leaves are supremely edible and are eaten both raw and cooked.

I have been unable to locate any information about its flowers or fruits.

PISTACIA

Pistachio
* **Deciduous/fast**
* **Edible nuts/** C
   autumn colour
* **Ht: 7-25m/21-75ft** T

Species of the small genus **Pistacia** are found in many places around the temperate Northern Hemisphere, on all continents. They take their name from *pistake,* a word the Greeks had for the succulent nuts borne by the European species, **P. vera.** These are still popular cocktail snacks in all countries, and they ripen on a small 7m tree.

Far more commonly grown all over the world is its oriental cousin, **P. chinensis,** a much larger tree which may reach 25m in a suitable position. It is one of the most widely planted trees for autumn colour. The glossy leaves begin to turn quite early in cool climates, developing a veritable rainbow of tints ranging from yellow to scarlet, with an occasional patch of purple. The colour persists for many weeks.

Pistachios enjoy full sun and are not particularly fussy about soil.

PITTOSPORUM

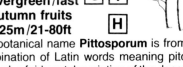

Mockorange, Tarata,
Native Daphne
  * **Evergreen**/fast [C] [T]
  * **Autumn fruits**
  * **7-25m/21-80ft** [H]

The botanical name **Pittosporum** is from a combination of Latin words meaning pitch-seeded, a fairly apt description of the decorative fruits which make them so popular in many parts of the great Pacific area where they are found and cultivated.

All are evergreens, mostly with shining, aromatic foliage, and a flower display more noted for its fragrance than startling appearance, the blooms varying from green through cream. But the fruits that follow are often brilliantly coloured — anywhere from bright yellow to orange, and when they ripen and split open, it is often to reveal a scarlet and black interior.

In a word, they are sticky, for the seed

Pittosporum eugenioides variegatum
Silver Tarata

Pittosporum rhombifolium
Queensland Pittosporum

PITTOSPORUM (continued)

capsules are full of a tacky resin with all the adhesive power of freshly laid asphalt.

All **Pittosporums** are members of the botanical family Pittosporaceae, and while widely scattered in nature, tend to centre on Australia and New Zealand, though some species are native to east Africa, South-East Asia and Hawaii. They are sturdy, fast-growing plants, mostly of tree size, and now popular for landscaping in warm-climate areas all over the world.

Popular species include the Japanese **P. tobira,** a shrubby tree with blunt-ended, leathery leaves and bright yellow fruit. This has a variegated-foliage form and both are widely planted in California.

Also with variegated leaves is New Zealand's **P. eugenioides variegatum,** the Silver Tarata, a handsome pyramidal tree with cream-edged grey-green leaves.

Popular Australian species include the Queensland Pittosporum, **P. rhombifolium,** a leggy 10m tree with dark rhomboid leaves and a show of orange autumn fruits that persist for months. Further south, in Victoria, they prize the Native Daphne, **P. undulatum,** which has pointed leaves of a distinctive pale green, and fragrant blossom followed by yellow-orange fruits.

All **Pittosporums** grow easily from seed, but they are best kept away from paths, where the fallen fruits become a nuisance.

Pittosporum tobira
Mockorange

Pittosporum undulatum
fruit detail

Platanus racemosa
Western Plane

PLATANUS

Plane, Sycamore   C

* **Deciduous /fast**
* **Ht: 20-50m /60-160ft** T

Most widely planted street tree in the world, the gracious London Plane, **Platanus** X **acerifolia** is propagated by the million. It satisfies all the criteria for life in the big city, growing tall and fast, spreading strong and wide, and presenting a decorative appearance at all times of the year.

The London Plane is a hybrid between two original species, the Chinar (**P. orientalis**) from Asia, and the Buttonwood (**P. occidentalis**) from the USA. It has the heat resistance of one and the cold-hardiness of the other. It can easily reach 25m in a good rich soil, and I have one in my own garden that shot up to 10m in six years and spread almost as wide. The London Plane is of

Platanus X acerifolia
London Plane

Platanus orientalis insularis
Cyprus Plane

PLATANUS (continued)

course deciduous, dropping the deposit of a year's atmospheric pollution with its leaves every autumn. It takes readily to shaping, and has remarkable powers of healing over the scars of lopped branches in no time.

The Chinar, **P. orientalis,** is the great tree of near-East gardens, seen to perfection in the Vale of Kashmir. Its leaves are more deeply lobed than those of the London Plane, and in the variety **P. o. insularis,** the Cyprus Plane, the lobes are cut almost to the stem.

In California and Mexico the Sycamore, **P. racemosa,** is more often seen. A slightly smaller tree, with a slimmer trunk often picturesquely twisted in exposed positions, its deeply lobed leaves are thick, with distinctly woolly reverses. It is the best species for dryish soils and climates.

Platanus is from the Greek *platys* meaning flat. All species strike easily from cuttings.

PODOCARPUS

Fern Pine, Yellowwood,
Podocarp, Totara
 * **Evergreen /fast**
 * **Summer fruit**
 * **Ht: 20-50m /60-160ft** $\boxed{\text{T}}$ $\boxed{\text{H}}$

Though fairly widespread in nature, the graceful coniferous genus **Podocarpus** is relatively unknown to the cooler climate gardeners of the Northern Hemisphere, except in China and Japan, where the dark-leafed Buddhist Pines, **P. macrophyllus** and **P. nagi,** are very much part of the ornamental landscape.

But in the Southern Hemisphere they really come into their own, for the principal species are natives of South America, New Zealand and South Africa. They are the only conifers found naturally in the southern half of the African continent, and are known there as Fern Pines or Yellowwood. **Podocarpus**

are related more to the Yews than the Pines, and their fruits, while technically cones, look more like a large berry sitting on a fat stalk. The botanical name **Podocarpus** in fact means footed stalk.

In South Africa several species are among the most important timber trees. These are: **P. elongatus,** the African Yellowwood, a 25m tree with fine, 5cm needle leaves and green fruits on red stalks; **P. falcatus,** the Oteniqua Yellowwood, a large tree that may reach 50m with thin, shedding bark, leaves are as little as 2mm wide, and bluish-green or yellow fruit; finally, **P. latifolius,** a 30m tree, also has blue-green fruits, and coarser leaves 5mm in width.

Further north, the Fern Pine, **P. gracilior,** is found in Kenya, Uganda and Ethiopia. It rarely tops 20m, bears striking purple fruits and is widely grown in southern California.

New Zealand species are rarely seen outside that country, but are among the most impressive. They include: the Totara, **P.**

Podocarpus falcatus
fruit detail

115

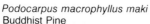

Podocarpus gracilior
Fern Pine

PODOCARPUS (continued)

totara, a 30m giant with green fruits on red stalks; the New Zealand White Pine, **P. dacrydioides,** which may reach 50m and has bronze-green fruits on reddish stalks; the Maki or Black Pine, **P. spicata,** also from New Zealand, has black fruits without the typical stalk.

The principal South American species are: **P. andinus,** the Plum-fruited Yew, with pale yellow fruits; and **P. salignus,** which grows to 20m, with weeping branches.

The species **P. nerifolia** is more tropical in origin, ranging from Japan to Borneo, and is widely grown in Hawaii, the Philippines and other warm places. It grows to 20m, has much larger dark leaves, and very small green fruits.

None of the genus is really frost-hardy; all of them can be grown from seeds or summer cuttings, and they are most attractive trees in the temperate garden, having generally a wide-branched, spreading shape.

Podocarpus macrophyllus maki
Buddhist Pine

Podocarpus macrophyllus angustifolia
Kusamaki

116

POPULUS

Poplar, Cottonwood,
Aspen, Balsam
 * **Deciduous /fast**   ☐C
 * **Autumn colour**
 * **Ht: 13-45m /40-140ft**   ☐T

I doubt if it had occurred to me before I began serious research for this book, separating old gardener's fancy from cold botanical fact, just how closely the Poplars resemble the Willows (see **Salix**). They are both included in the family Salicaceae, to be sure, but one's thinking is so clouded by the appearance of the tall, spire-like Lombardy Poplar (**P. nigra** 'Italica'). And yet the Lombardy Poplar (a hybrid cultivar) is the most untypical of all Poplars, resembling only the upright Humboldt Willow **(Salix humboldtii)** among the whole Willow family.

Like Willows, the Poplars are waterside plants, sharing a terrible thirst and a predilection for the banks of streams and low, waterlogged ground on which they grow quicker than any other genus of tree. They are native to all continents of the Northern Hemisphere, where they are generally found in cool, temperate areas.

The Willow relationship appears again in the colourful catkins of spring blossom produced at the leaf axils. The fertilized catkins of many species produce a mass of seeds tangled in cottony thread. American species are popularly known as Cottonwood from this characteristic.

Species from all continents grow easily from cuttings, and rapidly form dense thickets from root suckers. For garden use, they are normally grafted on non-suckering stock.

Commonly seen species include:
From Asia:

The White Poplar, **P. alba,** with smooth grey bark and white-backed leaves, deeply cut. It is rarely grown as a specimen due to its suckering habit.

The Grey Poplar, **P. canescens,** same size as **P. alba,** leaves less deeply cut.

The China Poplar, **P. lasiocarpa,** a smaller tree with very large leaves which have red veins and leaf stalks.

P. simoni 'Fastigiata', similar to the Lombardy Poplar, but smaller and with reddish leaf stalks.

P. yunnanensis, the Chinese Poplar, with shiny, tapered leaves, slightly red veins.

Populus nigra italica
Lombardy Poplar

Populus deltoides
Cottonwood

117

Populus alba
White Poplar

POPULUS (continued)

From North America:
The Cottonwood, **P. deltoides;** triangular dark-green leaves and red catkins.

From Fremont Cottonwood, **P. fremontii,** a gigantic round-topped tree to 30m.

The Western Balsam Poplar, **P. trichocarpa,** tallest of all, to 70m; broad shiny leaves with white reverses.
From Europe:
The Black Poplar, **P. nigra,** parent of the Italian species, leaves triangular.

The Golden Poplar, **P. serotina** 'Aurea', a hybrid sometimes known as **P. X canadensis.**

The Aspen, **P. tremula,** has a bad suckering habit. The leaves seem in a constant state of motion due to a peculiarity in their stalk structure.

Many Poplar species are known as Balsams.

Populus X *canadensis*
Golden Poplar

Populus trichocarpa
Black Cottonwood

Prunus serrulata
Japanese Cherry

PRUNUS

Peach, Plum, Cherry,
Apricot, etc.
* **Deciduous/fast**
* **Summer fruit**
* **Ht: 7-23m/21-75m** C T

The hundreds of **Prunus** species are members of the Rose family, and they all bear flowers with a passing resemblance to Roses. But it takes a really creative imagination to spot the relationship between, say, a flowering Cherry **(P. serrulata)** and an evergreen Cherry Laurel **(P. laurocerasus)**, though they are more closely related to each other than to any different genus of plants.

For horticultural purposes, one has to make a totally artificial division of this very large genus — over 200 species and probably upwards of 2000 cultivars — all of them from the Northern Hemisphere. That division

is between the species grown for the delight of the appetite, and the others grown purely for eye appeal.

To take them in that order, the popular edible species include: the Apricot, **Prunus armeniaca;** the Cherry, **P. cerasus;** the Plum, **P. domestica;** the Almond, **P. dulcis;** the Peach, **P. persica,** together with a host of minor species with local popularity such as the American Red Plum, **P. americana;** the Gean, **P. avium;** the Cherry Plum, **P. cerasifera;** the Greengages and Damsons, **P. institia;** the St Lucie Cherry, **P. mahaleb;** the Japanese Plum, **P. salicina;** the Sloe, **P. spinosa;** and the Almond Cherry, **P. triloba.**

Most of these are to one degree or another bushy trees, rarely above 5m. They need a deal of pruning or shaping to produce a satisfactory fruit crop. They are all deciduous, with attractive, single rose-type flowers in early spring. These appear generally on small spur-like branchlets designed to take

119

Prunus domestica
Plum

Prunus cerasus
Cherry

PRUNUS (continued)

the weight of the fruit. All fruiting species may be grown from their seeds or stones, but are generally propagated by bud grafting to be certain of variety and quality.

Away from the kitchen garden or orchard, there is a vast range of ornamental species, grown purely for their blossom. Some are sterile, others bear an occasional fruit.

By far the most popular group of ornamentals are the Japanese Flowering Cherries, mostly hybrids of **P. serrulata** with a number of other oriental species.

In Western gardens, the spring display is provided more by a range of flowering peaches, hybrids of **P. amygdalus,** the Flowering Almond, **P. persica,** the Peach,

and **P. glandulosa,** the flowering Almond-Cherry.

Finally, there are a number of less common evergreen species grown as much for the beauty of their foliage as for their generally white blossom. They are sometimes pruned as hedges, or certain low-growing species are used as ground covers. The evergreen types include: the Californian **P. ilicifolia;** the Versailles or Cherry Laurel, **P. laurocerasus;** and the Portugal Laurel, **P. lusitanica;** all are small growing.

In cooler climates many of the fruiting **Prunus** species are espaliered to make the most of warm, sunward-facing walls and ensure maximum cropping. Others, like **P. maackii,** are grown for the beauty of their peeling bark in cold weather.

Prunus persica
Peach 'White Shanghai'

Prunus armeniaca
Apricot

PSIDIUM

Guavas
* **Evergreen/fast**
* **Summer fruits**
* **Ht: 8-10m/25-30ft** [T]   [H]

Though native only to the warmer parts of Central and South America, the many Guava species have spread around the globe to become perhaps the most widely grown of tropical fruits outside the Banana and Mango. The secret of their popularity lies, perhaps, in their ease of growth, for they are no trouble to propagate from cuttings, and naturalize readily once established. They are also remarkably unfussy as to climate, flourishing from the full tropics to areas with a few degrees of frost.

Over a hundred separate species have been listed, though only three are commonly seen away from the Americas. These are:

P. cattleianum, the Purple or Cherry Guava, a slim, leggy tree of perhaps 8m with smooth, reddish bark. Evergreen, it bears dark, leathery leaves very much like those of the related **Tristania** (see Tristania). The flowers are white, solitary, rather like Eucalypt blossoms. The summer fruits are purple-red and cherry sized. They are eaten raw, or more often made into jams and jellies.

Less popular is the closely related Yellow Strawberry Guava, **P. cattleianum littorale** which is more heavily branched and bears larger orange-yellow fruits.

This tree should not be mistaken however for the universally grown **P. guajava,** the common Apple Guava or Yellow Guava. This is a larger, heavier tree, to 10m high, with scaly bark and prominently veined downy leaves up to 15cm in length. The white flowers appear in small clusters, and the pink-fleshed yellow-skinned fruits are the size of a small peach. They are the source of commercial Guava juice, and have a rather peculiar odour.

Guava is the native South American name. The botanical **Psidium** is from the old Greek word for Pomegranate, *psidion*.

All species are unfortunately subject to fruit-fly attack in infested areas, and must be sprayed regularly.

Psidium cattleianum
Cherry Guava

Guava, fruit detail

Pyrus communis
Common Pear

PYRUS

Pear
* **Deciduous /slow**
* **Summer fruit**
* **Ht: 10-20m /30-65ft**

C
T

We all believe blind Freddie could tell the difference between an apple and a pear, but until recent times many trees we now know as Quince, Medlar and Crabapple were classed, with many others, as Pears, or botanically speaking as **Pyrus** species, *pyrus* being the old Roman name.

Pears are not necessarily 'pear-shaped'. Sometimes they are round, sometimes flatter than round, like a tomato. Although their white flowers look similar to those of the Apples they have a different structure and the stalks of pear fruits are thicker than apple stalks, and do not join onto the fruit in a hollow. They are sort-of streamlined in.

Pears grow wild in Europe, Asia and Africa, but not in America. The flavour of most Pear species is distinctive, and they have a woody, granular texture when eaten, unless extremely ripe.

The leaves of some species are rounder and shinier than those of an apple, more like a Poplar's perhaps. But not all species. The foliage of **P. salicifolia,** the lovely Willow-leaf Pear from Asia Minor, is long, greyish and covered all over with silver-silky hair.

The Indian Pear, **P. pashia,** has toothed dark leaves and speckled round fruit.

The European Wild Pear, **P. communis,** is the ancestor of all the Pears we grow for the table. It has varieties with fruits of many colours.

Pears are propagated from seed, or by grafting of cultivated varieties on wild pear stock. They are frost-hardy, and do best in a fully sunny position in well-drained soil.

122

QUERCUS

Oak
* **Mostly deciduous /
  slow**
* **Autumn colour,
  acorns**
* **Ht: 17-40m /50-120ft** C T

The first tree I ever planted was an Oak —
well, an acorn anyway. My grandfather used
to tell me 'tall oaks from little acorns grow',
and I wanted to prove the unbelievable for
myself. Miraculously, in spite of being dug up
a number of times to check for progress, it did
sprout, it did grow; and for all I know it is still
growing: Oaks like to take their time.

The Oak I planted was an English Oak,
Quercus robur, often seen as a street tree in
Melbourne, where I spent much of my child-
hood, and very popular with the squirrels
which have migrated to that city.

In popular conversation, Oaks are often
used as yardsticks of comparison for a
number of desirable qualities like strength,
perseverance and age; all with good
reason.

There are some 450 species of Oak in
nature: some deciduous, some evergreen;
some tall, some spreading; some shrubby,
others among the largest of trees. Most have
the broad, rippled, many-lobed leaves like
the English species; others are dark and
shiny as holly, or slim and flimsy as a willow.

But what they all have in common is
acorns. The acorn, of course, is a large seed
or nut set in a cup. Some are long and
pointed, some flattened and squat; some
have hairy cups and some are smooth, but
they are all acorns.

Oaks in general prefer deep, mellow,
woodsy soil, and the leaves of deciduous
species break down into the most wonderful
humus of all for potting, and for feeding
acid-loving plants.

The timber of many Oak species has been
used in ship-building for thousands of years,
and is noted for its resistance to water and
most pests that destroy wood. From the six-
teenth to the nineteenth century, entire
forests of England, France and Spain were
denuded of old trees in the race for European
naval supremacy.

Before the introduction of exotic tropical
cabinet woods such as mahogany, oak was
used for long-lasting country furniture.

Quercus acutissima
Bristle-tipped Oak

Quercus borealis
acorn detail

Quercus borealis
Red Oak

QUERCUS (continued)

The botanical name **Quercus** has been used for the Oaks since Roman times, and they are classified in the same botanical family as the Beech trees, Fagaceae.

Oaks are found naturally all over the Northern Hemisphere and popular cultivated species include:

Q. acutissima, the Japanese Bristle-tipped Oak, with long, pointed bristle-toothed foliage; it grows to 17m.

Q. agrifolia, the California Live Oak, evergreen, and growing to 35m.

Q. borealis, the American Red Oak, 27m, with gorgeous autumn colouring.

Q. ilex, the Mediterranean Holly Oak, 20m and with dark, evergreen foliage, woolly beneath.

Q. palustris, the American Pin Oak, to 40m; magnificent autumn colour.

Q. robur, the English Oak; a squat, broad tree growing to 35m.

Q. suber, the Cork Oak, a north African species grown for its bark, from which cork is stripped.

Quercus myrsinaefolia
Evergreen Oak

Quercus agrifolia
Coast Live Oak

Quercus palustris
Pin Oak

Quercus robur
English Oak

Rhus succedanea
Wax Tree

Rhus typhina laciniata
Stag's Horn Sumach

RHUS

Sumach, Toxicodendron,
Wax Tree, Varnish Tree
* **Deciduous /fast**
* **Autumn colour /** [C]
  poisonous
* **Ht: 10-20m /30-60ft** [T]

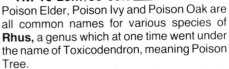

Poison Elder, Poison Ivy and Poison Oak are
all common names for various species of
Rhus, a genus which at one time went under
the name of Toxicodendron, meaning Poison
Tree.

If you detect a certain repetitive quality in
those names it is with good reason, for most
of the species, which number about 150,
have poisonous properties which can be
most umpleasant to some people — I em-
phasize, only *some* people. The botanical
name **Rhus** which is currently adopted, was
the original Greek name for European members of the genus.

Most commonly seen is the lovely, but
sparsely branched **Rhus succedanea** or
Wax Tree, from China and Japan. This grows
rapidly to 10m in a cool to warm temperate
climate, producing leaflets sometimes with a
purplish hue when young, and colouring to an
incredibly rich red in autumn. The yellowish
flowers hang in panicles from the leaf-axils,
and are followed by larger hanging clusters of
cherry-sized fruits. These are not edible, but
are a useful source of wax. It is an open,
sparsely branched tree.

The Stag's Horn Sumach, **R. typhina** CV
'Laciniata', from the eastern USA, is smaller,
rarely above 7m, and has magnificently
toothed foliage of a vivid lime green. This
turns a vivid red, orange and even purple in
the autumn.

The sap of **R. verniciflua,** the Lacquer
Tree, from China and Japan, is the base of all
oriental lacquer work. Like the related Wax
Tree, its yellow fruit is the source of a valuable wax used in candle making. **R. verniciflua** grows to 20m, has compound leaves
with up to 15 oval leaflets 20cm long. It must
be grown in pairs to develop the small
yellow fruits, turns a brilliant red in autumn.

Propagation of **Rhus** species is no problem, as they seem to self-seed all over the
place, but cuttings can be taken and struck
with care.

Their riotous display of autumn leaf colour
is best in a sheltered sunny position.

Robinia CV 'Frisia'
Golden Locust

ROBINIA

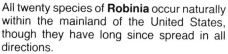

Black Locust
 * **Deciduous /fast** C
 * **Autumn colour**
 * **Ht: 20-27m /60-85ft** T

All twenty species of **Robinia** occur naturally within the mainland of the United States, though they have long since spread in all directions.

They are generally thorny members of the pea family, Leguminosae, with fragrant pea-type flowers, and dangling pods. The pods led to the popular name Black Locust,

as they resembled those of the related Locust Tree (see **Ceratonia**).

The commonly seen and frequently naturalized species is **R. pseudacacia,** normally a tall tree with dark gnarled trunk and frequently picturesque branches.

For garden usage, attractive cultivars have been developed from it, including: CV 'Fastigiata', with a tall, poplar-like shape, and the gorgeous 'CV Frisia', which has scarlet spines and foliage of an almost fluorescent golden green.

Foliage of all **Robinia** species turns a pale gold before leaf fall. They are propagated from seed or suckers.

SALIX

Willow, Osier, Sally
* **Deciduous / very fast** C T
* **Autumn colour**
* **Ht: 12-35m /36-110ft**

Think of water, think of willows! What country stream would be the same without their gnarled old trunks to frame its rippling chatter? Try to picture the edge of any lake without waterbirds playing hide-and-seek among the fine screens of weeping greenery.

The Weeping Willow, **Salix babylonica,** is so much a part of our landscapes, who'd believe it has only shared them since the eighteenth century, when it was imported from China? It is a great survivor. Just stick a twig or branch in damp soil, or even lay it in a pool of water, and you've a new tree in a matter of weeks. That, we believe, is how they spread about the world, from willow whips discarded by caravan drivers, woven willow baskets left along the way, broken branches carried downstream by a storm.

The world is full of Willow species (over 250 of them, mostly in the cooler Northern Hemisphere) and all share the love of water. They are invaluable for preventing erosion of river banks, or soaking up the brackish moisture of low meadows. They are also adept at seeking out and filling water pipes and blocking drains and do not have very civilized manners in the home garden.

Salix discolor
Pussy Willow

Salix matsudana CV 'Tortuosa'
Corkscrew Willow

Species from almost any part of the world hybridize indiscriminately, and it is probable that most of the ones we see and love are natural hybrids of some sort. Among them are:

S. alba, the White Willow of Europe and northern Asia. This is a most variable plant, appearing in one place as a thickly branched shrub, in another as a 25m tree with massive trunk. The long slim leaves have silver reverses.

S. babylonica, the Weeping Willow. A wide-crowned tree up to 15m with markedly weeping branches. Will grow in hot, dry climates by permanent water.

S. fragilis, the Crack Willow. A giant European tree of up to 30m, much cultivated for its timber. Similar leaves to the Weeping Willow, but without the weeping habit.

S. discolor, the Pussy Willow. A thirsty

SALIX (continued)

plant with voracious roots, but otherwise ideal for growing in damp, low-lying ground. Its branches point upward, the leaves are oval, and it is often grown for the beauty of its silver, furry catkins.

S. humboldtii, the Humboldt Willow from Chile, a tall, poplar-like tree with even narrower leaves than the Weeping Willow; grows to 10m.

S. matsudana CV 'Tortuosa', the Corkscrew Willow from China, is suited to positions with less water. Every part of the tree is twisted corkscrew fashion, from the trunk to the tips of the finest twigs. Its leaves are like those of the Weeping Willow, but it has a generally upright habit.

Willows are all deciduous, and bear their flowers in the form of catkins, sometimes long and drooping, sometimes short and plump, and usually with the male and female flowers on separate trees.

Many of the larger Willows are grown commercially as a timber crop, for they reach felling size very quickly. The wood is generally whitish, tough and brittle. Other species are valued for the slim twigs or withes which are woven into baskets, screens and wicker furniture.

For cold-climate gardens, there are species worth seeking out for the brilliant colouring of their winter bark — gold, scarlet, even purple.

Salix humboldtii
Humboldt Willow

Salix alba
White Willow

◄ *Salix babylonica*
Weeping Willow

129

Samanea saman
Monkeypod

SAMANEA

Monkeypod, Rain Tree
* **Semi-deciduous/ fast**
* **Pinnate foliage**
* **Ht: to 25m/80ft**

Should you ever be caught in a tropical downpour, do not head for shelter under the nearest Monkeypod Tree! These genial

Sapium sebiferum
Chinese Tallow Tree

South American giants fold their leaves at the first kiss of the raindrops, and let it all fall through!

It is perhaps this quality more than any other that has endeared them to warm-climate gardeners, for their spreading branches shade exotic orchids and other tropical epiphytes without robbing them of precious rainwater. The fern-like foliage is scantily borne just at the tips of branches, giving a light, dappled shade at all times. The leaves close up in the evening to let the dew fall, and drop themselves in winter to let the short day sunlight through.

A popular name in many areas is Rain Tree, but botanically it is called **Samanea saman,** and produces colourful tufts of blossom all through late spring and summer, followed by green and black pods full of sticky pulp and seeds. The beautifully figured wood is used for many decorative purposes.

Monkey Pods grow easily from seed, reaching their full height in a very few years.

SAPIUM

Chinese Tallow Tree
* **Deciduous/fast**
* **Autumn colour/ white berries**
* **Ht: to 8m/25ft**

C
T
H

Rarely more than 8m high in cultivation, the

130

charming Chinese Tallow Tree **(Sapium sebiferum)** is widely cultivated in temperate to tropical areas, and has become naturalized in parts of the United States.

It has a dense, many-branched habit, and in cooler climates the drooping top-shaped leaves rarely exceed 5cm in length.

Small yellowish flowers appear in terminal spikes during early summer, followed by 1cm fruiting capsules which consist of three seeds, each covered with a white vegetable wax. This is used for soap and candle-making in its native Far East, but in Western countries the tree is grown purely as an ornamental.

In marginal warm-temperate areas, where the autumn colour of many other trees cannot be relied on, the Tallow Tree turns a wonderful mixture of red and bronze. Against this flaming background, the white, wax-coated seeds make a brilliant and unusual contrast.

Sassafras albidum
Sassafras

Schinus areira
Peppercorn Tree

SASSAFRAS

(No popular name)
* **Deciduous /fast**
* **Aromatic bark /**
   autumn colour
* **Ht: to 18m /60ft**

| C |

| T |

Found naturally right down the east coast of the United States from Maine to Florida, deciduous **Sassafras albidum** is cultivated for its showy but variable autumn colour, which may be yellow, orange or red in any particular year. It likes a well-drained, acid soil with plenty of moisture; suffers badly in drought or long, hot summers. All parts of the tree have a pleasant, aromatic fragrance, and oil of sassafras (used in flavouring many medications) is extracted from the bark, which is also sometimes ground and used as a herb tea. The foliage is unique and variable: individual leaves may be simple and oval, fully three-lobed or anything in between. Small racemes of greenish yellow flowers appear in spring, followed by inedible fruits. **Sassafras** grows rapidly to 8m, then slows down. A decorative specimen for any climate.

SCHINUS

Peppercorn Tree, Mastic,
Christmas Berry
* **Evergreen/fast**
* **Decorative berries**
* **Ht: 7-17m/21-55ft**

Wherever the climate is dry and warm (Australia, California, South Africa, the Mediterranean), you'll find the picturesque Peppercorn Tree, **Schinus areira,** known variously as Pepperina, California Pepper Tree, Pirul and Peruvian Mastic. It is a native of Peru's Andean deserts, grows happily in arid, sandy soil of any temperate area, and quickly becomes the most decorative of shade trees. The leaves are bluish-green, each carrying up to thirty stemless leaflets, and they hang from delicate weeping branchlets.

Peppercorn trees produce clusters of tiny creamy-yellow flowers which are followed (on female trees only) by chains of round, rosy-pink peppercorns. These are not the peppercorns of commerce, but are often mixed with them in blends.

A related and more colourful species is the Christmas Berry or Brazilian Mastic Tree, **S. terebinthifolius,** quite without the grace of the Peppercorn. The leaflets are coarser and dark green, and the flowers are white, and borne in upright spikes. The berries that follow are larger, and vary from deep pink to a vivid scarlet; they are the pink peppercorns of commerce. All parts of the tree are fragrant with a volatile, spicy oil.

Both species of **Schinus** are propagated from seed and naturalize readily.

Schinus areira
fruit detail

Schinus terebinthifolius
Brazilian Mastic

SCIADOPITYS

Umbrella Pine
* **Evergreen/slow**
* **Decorative conifer**
* **Ht: to 10m/30ft**

You can be sure some talented modern designer would have invented **Sciadopitys** if it did not already grow wild in the mountains of Japan.

Unbelievably formal, a perfect cone with needle-like leaves arranged exactly like the spokes of an umbrella, it is not common in cultivation because it refuses to grow in pol-

SCIADOPITYS (continued)

luted air. But give it a sheltered spot in mountain soil, and you have a thing of beauty, a joy forever.

Plant it out when very young and do not disturb for a generation or two except for an annual top-dressing with compost.

Sciadopitys verticillata likes water, but not wet feet, and sunlight, but not hot sun, for its surface roots dry out easily.

Given time, it will reach 10m, but it may surprise your descendants, for it has been measured at 40m in the wild in Japan.

Its common name is the Umbrella Pine.

SEQUOIA

California Redwood
* **Evergreen/fast** C
* **Decorative conifer**
* **Ht: to 40m/120ft** T

Sciadopitys verticillata
Umbrella Pine

Sequoia sempervirens
California Redwood

Though there may have been taller trees in Australia in the nineteenth century, the tallest today are America's noble Redwoods or **Sequoias.** In misty coastal forests of northern California they huddle protectively together as if seeking safety in numbers.

For the fast-growing California or Coastal Redwood is one of the world's great timber trees, its fragrant trunkwood soft and light yet almost impervious to weather. Naturally a rich, rosy red, it will weather gradually to a soft, silvery grey.

Called botanically by the lovely old Indian name **Sequoia,** the Redwood grows easily from seed, or from the shoots that sprout from dormant buds or burls around the base of felled trees.

The Redwood's trunk is straight and fissured, the needle-like leaves arranged in flattened layers like the related Swamp Cypress (see **Taxodium**). The cones are oval and woody, about the size of a grape.

Sequoia sempervirens is rather less cold-resistant than the closely related **Sequoiadendron,** and because of its habit of growing in dense groves, more difficult to cultivate unless it can be given the shelter of other trees, at least in its early stages.

Even young **Sequoias** are inclined to throw suckers from around the trunk. These should be removed as quickly as possible to give the main trunk a chance.

SEQUOIADENDRON

Big Tree, Giant Sequoia
* **Evergreen /fast**
* **Persistent cones**
* **Ht: to 85m /250ft**

C

T

May the king live forever! The king of trees just has to be majestic **Sequoiadendron,** the Big Tree or Giant Sequoia of California. Immense in size, immense in age, there are individual trees living in California's Sierra Mountains that were thousands of years old when Christ was born.

Unlike the related **Sequoias,** they are loners, growing individually among mixed forests of other coniferous trees. They have taken well to culture as single specimens in parks and large gardens of many temperate lands, where they actually seem to grow faster than in the wild.

Sequoiadendron giganteum is raised from seed (or grafted cuttings) and grows straight as a die: a perfect, formal pyramid with horizontal, tapered branches and wonderful thick, red bark. The tiny scale-like leaves are arranged spirally on fine terminal twigs and have a silvery sheen. The greenish cones, very small for such a large tree, are rarely above the size of a grape.

The Big Tree is of course frost-hardy, and very worthwhile planting for its good garden manners and stunning vertical effect. There are good specimens in botanic gardens of several Australian cities, and in parks all over Europe.

Their ultimate height (as measured in California) is somewhat less than that of the **Sequoia,** but the trunk is much thicker and heavily buttressed. The trunk is in effect its main feature, for some famous trees in the wild do not have a single branch below 30m from the ground.

At one time, there was an attempt to name the tree Washingtonia, after America's first President; but the name had already been given to a Californian Palm. The English, in a burst of post-Napoleonic euphoria, countersuggested that the name of the Hero of Waterloo might be used as Wellingtonia. That idea went down in America like a lead balloon!

So **Sequoiadendron** it is and **Sequoiadendron** it will remain.

Sequoiadendron giganteum
Big Tree

Sequoiadendron
foliage detail

SORBUS

Mountain Ash, Whitebeam,
Service Berry, Rowan
* **Deciduous /fast**
* **Summer /fruits** $\boxed{C}$ $\boxed{T}$
* **Ht: 10-20m /30-60ft**

Is there no end to the showy, fruit-bearing
genera of the Rose family? After reading
about the Apples, Apricots, Cherries, Haw-
thorns, Loquats, Medlars, Peaches, Plums
and Quinces you might think that we'd done
our dash, but no, there's still one of the most
important Rose genera of all. **Sorbus** is the
botanical name, but you'll probably recog-
nize one or more of them better under their
popular names of Mountain Ash, Rowan,
Whitebeam or Service Berry.

They are all from cool temperate regions of
the Northern Hemisphere and grow wild in
North America, Europe, and northern Asia;
but in the cooler Southern Hemisphere you
find them only as treasured garden specimens.

The Rowan or Mountain Ash **(Sorbus aucuparia)** will probably be the most familiar. It
is a tree of up to 20m in forests all over
Europe and the Caucasus; a handsome, slim
grower with ash-like compound leaves of up
to fifteen elongated leaflets. The early spring
flowers are white, like Hawthorn. The 1cm
summer fruits are vivid scarlet and hang in
large clusters all over the tree. If the birds
leave them alone they'll still be there right up
to the time that autumn turns the whole tree a
brilliant golden yellow.

The American Mountain Ash, **S.
americana,** is very similar, but smaller in all
its parts.

Also from Europe is the Service Berry or **S.
domestica,** a more recognizably tree-
shaped plant, reaching 27m in the wild. Deciduous, its leaves are coarser with up to
twenty-one leaflets. The fruits are 3cm in
diameter, and pale red. In Europe they are
sometimes eaten when overripe, or brewed
into a type of cider.

The Whitebeam, **S. aria,** is European as
well, but a totally different type of tree, heavily
clothed with single, toothed leaves of a rather
long shape. It has clusters of white, cherry-
blossom sized flowers, followed by masses
of long-stemmed oblong fruits that ripen from
green to scarlet. The Whitebeam grows to
17m high and has a particularly showy vari-

Sorbus aucuparia
Mountain Ash

Sorbus mougiottii
Alpine Whitebeam

Sterculia quadrifida
Scarlet Sterculia

Sterculia foetida
Java Olive

SORBUS (continued)

ety, **S.a. majestica,** on which the leaves are neatly pleated.

The Swedish Whitebeam, **S. intermedia,** has rounder, double-toothed leaves and smaller red fruits. It is a good tree for an exposed position, and the tough wood is used to manufacture a number of small articles.

S. mougiottii is a smaller, more spectacular tree from the European Alps and the Pyrenees. Its bronzy, toothed leaves are backed with silver grey and the large orange-red fruits are borne in long, hanging clusters.

Among the Asiatic species, **S. pekingensis** is particularly attractive. Its pinnate, compound leaves are deep purple-crimson on scarlet stems. The flowers are white, the small fruit a vivid scarlet. It grows to about 10m.

All eighty-five **Sorbus** species do best in cooler areas, preferably in a sunny, sheltered position. They are easily propagated from berries and many of them make stunning street trees.

There are many cultivars with coloured leaves, and also a number of variations in berry colour — white, pink, yellow and orange. These are propagated by grafting.

The botanical name **Sorbus** was an old Latin word for the fruit of the Service Berry.

STERCULIA

Skunk Tree, Java Olive
* **Deciduous /fast**
* **Summer fruit**
* **Ht: 7-20m /21-60ft** [T] [H]

Related to Australia's Kurrajongs and Booyongs, the **Sterculias** are a large tree genus, mostly from warm-climate areas of Asia. At one time the Kurrajongs were included among them, until reclassified as a genus of their own (see **Brachychiton**).

Useless for their timber, which is soft and light, they are planted only for shade and ornament. Most commonly seen is the Java Olive or Indian Almond, **S. foetida,** a large tree of 20m with large palmate leaves of five or seven lobes. The small orange flowers

STERCULIA (continued)

appear in panicles and have an unpleasant odour; in fact the tree's botanical name is derived from *stercus,* the Latin word for dung. The seeds are sometimes roasted and eaten.

South China's **S. lanceolata** is often seen in Hong Kong where its star-shaped clusters of seed pods are greatly admired as they change from green to a brilliant scarlet. It is small (rarely exceeding 6m) with simple oval leaves, rather like those of a Persimmon, and unspectacular green and pink flowers. It needs a sunny position to produce full colour in its pods.

In Central America, a common species called **S. apetala** is known as the Panama Tree, and gave its name to that small republic. It bears large five-lobed, heart-shaped leaves, small yellowish flowers and again, the seed capsules are divided into five parts, just like **S. lanceolata.**

In north-eastern Australia grows the roughtly pyramidal **S. quadrifida,** in which the colourful boat-shaped seed pods are arranged in the form of a four-pointed star. It is very fast growing with single, roughly heart-shaped leaves.

Sterculias are strictly for the warmer climate, and prefer a sunny, sheltered position with deep soil.

Swietenia mahagoni
Spanish Mahogany

Swietenia macrophylla
Honduras Mahogany

SWIETENIA

Mahogany
  * **Evergreen /fast**
  * **Autumn colour**
  * **Ht: 25-50m /75-160ft**

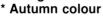
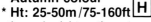

In the early eighteenth century, the discovery of a new genus of timber tree in the Caribbean area was to revolutionize English cabinet-making. Although the genus was small, the trees themselves were towering giants of up to 50m in the forests of Honduras, with heavy trunks of hard straight-grained timber coloured a rich red-brown. Seasoned properly, and cut with the grain, it could be made into furniture with a finish like glowing satin.

The trees were christened **Swietenia,** after a Dutch botanist of the period, but the

Syncarpia glomulifera
Turpentine

Syncarpia
bark detail

exotic-sounding native name *mahagoni* was to catch European fancy and after a slight modification to Mahogany became immortalized by such famous designers as Chippendale, Sheraton, and Hepplewhite, who preferred it above all other woods for their finest work.

Today, the trees are planted all over the tropical world, for they propagate quite easily from cuttings.

Two species in particular are sought by the furniture makers of the world. **S. mahagoni,** the West Indies or Spanish Mahogany, is a scaly-barked tree of 25m found in many parts of the Caribbean from Florida southward. It has compound leaves with up to ten oval leaflets. Small white flowers appear at branch tips and are followed by woody 10cm fruit containing many winged seeds. It is planted as both a shade and a street tree in many warm-climate areas.

The related Honduras Mahogany, **S. macrophylla,** is the more valuable species in commerce, and requires a fully tropical climate to grow well. It may reach 50m in jungle conditions, has large compound leaves with up to twelve narrow leaflets, similar flowers, and larger seed pods. It is native to a hot, humid belt right down the Caribbean coast and well into the South American continent. Its timber is slightly easier to work, but furniture made from it seems no less durable.

The Mahoganies are both referred to as evergreen, but in Australia at least they colour well in autumn and shed almost all their foliage during the dry, tropical winter. Away from a tropical climate, however, they grow to only a fraction of their forest size.

SYNCARPIA

Turpentine
* **Evergreen /fast**
* **Decorative bark**
* **Ht: to 25m /80ft** T

Possibly the finest and most useful tree of Australia's east coast is the Turpentine, **Syncarpia glomulifera,** found in abundance in southern New South Wales. Often mista-

SYNCARPIA (continued)

ken for a Eucalypt (to which it is related) the Turpentine sends up a towering trunk as high as 25m.

This is particularly sought-after and cut for the valuable straight-grained, heavy pink timber, which is used in underwater construction. It is completely resistant to toredo and other marine borers due to its impregnation with a turpentine-scented resin.

The Turpentine's deeply ridged bark is thick and fibrous, the dark 9cm leaves tough and wavy, with silvery-grey reverses. Like Eucalypt blossom, the creamy white flowers are a mass of stamens and appear each spring. The big difference is they appear generally seven at a time, fused together on long stalks. When the stamens fall, there remains a multiple-celled seed capsule, rather like the head of a medieval war mace. These give the tree its name **Syncarpia,** meaning seeds together.

There is only one other tree in the genus, the larger-leafed Peebeen or **S. hillii,** found only on Queensland's Fraser Island.

Syncarpia is grown widely in the southern United States and Hawaii, as both a shade and a timber tree.

Syzygium paniculatum
Brush Cherry

SYZYGIUM

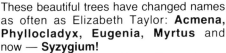

Lillypilly, Roseapple,
Jambolana, Java Plum
  * **Evergreen /fast**   [T]
  * **Summer fruits**
  * **Ht: 10-27m /30-85ft** [H]

Syzygium luehmannii
Water Myrtle

These beautiful trees have changed names as often as Elizabeth Taylor: **Acmena, Phyllocladyx, Eugenia, Myrtus** and now — **Syzygium!**

The latest division has all species of **Eugenia** from Africa, Asia and Australia classed as **Syzygium.** But they are still labelled **Eugenia** in most of the world's major botanic gardens and dictionaries of cultivated plants.

There are between four and five hundred species, all with glossy, evergreen foliage, and often brilliantly coloured new leaves. The flowers are almost all creamy-white, a mass of stamens, and are followed by vividly col-

Tamarindus indicus
Tamarind

Tamarind, fruit detail

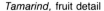

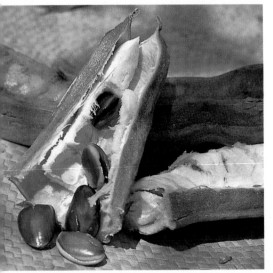

SYZYGIUM (continued)

oured fruits, often pink, and delicately sweet. They come from warm-temperate to tropical climates, enjoy humidity and are not very resistant to frost, at least when young.

Among the popularly grown species are:

S. aromaticum, from the Moluccas; this has clove-scented leaves and its buds are the cloves in your kitchen.

S. coolminianum, the Blue Lillypilly, from Australia.

S. cumini, the Java Plum or Jambolana, from Indo/Malaysia.

S. grande, the Sea Apple, from Thailand.

S. jambos, the Rose Apple or Jumbu.

S. floribundum, the Weeping Myrtle, Australian.

S. luehmannii, the Cherry Alder or Water Myrtle, Australian.

S. malaccense, the lovely Malay Apple, with purple-pink flowers.

S. paniculatum, Brush Cherry, Australia.

S. samarangense, the Java Apple or Jambool, Malaysia.

Most of the above are cultivated as specimen trees in warm-climate gardens throughout the world.

But **Syzygium?** I looked it up in my trusty Funk and Wagnalls and all that tells me is that a *syzygy* is the point of conjunction of two heavenly bodies. The connection eludes me, but the word is a sure winner for my next game of scrabble!

TAMARINDUS

Tamarind
* **Evergreen /fast**   T
* **Summer fruits**
* **Ht: to 25m /75ft**   H

'Ripe Dates from India' would be a reasonable translation of this useful tree's botanical name, borrowed from the Arabic *tamr-i-hind.* It would also describe the delicious, sticky pulp for which the tree is grown.

Tamarindus indicus is the only species in the genus, a slow-growing tree for the hot climate, whether wet or dry. Frequently seen in villages all over the tropics as a shade tree, it may reach 25m, and spread its branches nearly as wide. The evergreen compound

140

TAMARINDUS (continued)

leaves are fern-like, the small red and yellow pea flowers are not very showy, but the long strap-shaped pods are the tree's great feature.

They contain up to ten large seeds embedded in a thick, sticky pulp, rich in sugar and tartaric acid. The pulp is boiled and strained to make a delicious syrup used in all sorts of tropical drinks and curries. The dried pulp is sold at most Asian food stores.

TAXODIUM

Bald Cypress,
Swamp Cypress
* **Deciduous/fast** 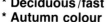 C T
* **Autumn colour**
* **Ht: 40-50m/125-160ft** H

Who can be unfamiliar with the North American Bald Cypress? Scarcely a month goes by on television without some mystery set among those ghostly conifers of the American swamps, their spreading branches festooned with eerie Spanish Moss.

Their botanical name is **Taxodium,** meaning 'like a Yew' (see **Taxus**), and they do have similarly-shaped leaves, but there the resemblance ends. **Taxodiums** are found only in North America. They are water-loving trees, found beside or actually in water, where they develop buttresses around the trunk, and curious conical projections called 'knees' which are raised above water level from outlying roots and enable the trees to breathe.

Taxodiums are deciduous, and develop great, spreading branches. Flowers are in the form of catkins, followed by small, scaly cones, 2.5cm long. Bald Cypress foliage is a delicious, fresh green throughout the warm weather, and the timber is much used for its water-resistant properties.

While they prefer marshy sites, **Taxodiums** will grow happily enough in a deep garden soil, are propagated from seed.

There are two species only:

T. distichum, Bald Cypress, native to the south-east United States.

T. mucronatum, Montezuma Cypress, from Mexico's Pacific coast.

Taxodium distichum
Bald Cypress

Taxodium, fruit detail

TAXUS

Yew
* **Evergreen/slow**
* **Red summer fruits**
* **Ht: to 27m/80ft**

$\boxed{C}$

$\boxed{T}$

One of the oldest trees in cultivation, and certainly one of the longest-lived, the Yew or **Taxus** is that anomaly, a conifer without cones.

To see a really big one, you'd have to visit old gardens or churchyards of the Northern Hemisphere, for they are so slow-growing that south of the Equator they just haven't had time to push much beyond shrub size. But take my word for it, they do grow big. One famous specimen in the Scottish Highlands measured over 17m in girth.

Yews have been around so long that the Romans borrowed their botanical name **Taxus** from the Ancient Greek. There are half a dozen species scattered about cooler areas of the Northern Hemisphere.

They are evergreen, with dark, narrow leaves modified almost to needle shape, and arranged spirally around the branchlets. The flowers appear in leaf-axils, male on one tree, female on another. The tiny male flowers are borne in clusters, and would not be noticeable except for the incredible amount of pollen they produce, scattering it far around. The female flower is a tiny green globule, which, when fertilized, expands into the fruit. This in itself is most eyecatching, a single green seed only partly covered by a succulent scarlet sheath or aril. The aril is the only part of the tree's structure that is not poisonous.

Only three cultivated varieties of the English or Irish Yew, **T. baccata,** are much grown. They are:
CV 'Aurea' with golden leaves;
CV 'Fastigiata' with a columnar habit;
CV 'Pendula', with long, weeping branches.

The original species **T. baccata** is a generally untidy-looking tree, somewhat pyramidal in youth, but later developing a spreading, horizontal crown, much like California's Monterey Cypress.

The hard wood has been used at various times for furniture-making, and of course for the famous English long-bows of medieval times. Propagated from ripe seed in spring, or from cuttings.

Taxus baccata
Irish Yew

Taxus baccata, fruit

TECTONA

Teak
* **Deciduous/fast**
* **Fine timber**
* **Ht: to 50m/160ft**

The towering Teak trees of South-East Asia shared their days of glory with the mighty windjammers. The trunks, straight as a die to 50m, were carved into masts that could support the fastest head of sail. Aged and sawn into planking, they became decks for the finest ships afloat.

Well, the days of sail have passed, and so have the largest of the Teak trees. What's left is now among the most expensive timber in the world, used for fine quality furniture and buildings that may last a thousand years.

Tectona grandis, as Teak is called by botanists, comes from *tekka,* the old name in South India; and it grows wild in monsoonal forests all over southern Asia. Due to its handsome foliage, Teak is often planted as an ornamental outside the truly tropical climate it needs for full development.

In late summer, the tree blossoms, producing great airy panicles of mauve and white flowers high on its topmost branches. These are followed by dry, papery brown fruits.

It is from these seeds that the Teak tree naturalizes in the tropics, but elsewhere it is propagated from shoots which grow at a great rate, up to 3m in two years.

Teakwood is heavier than water and will sink, so in Thailand the trees are ring-barked and left to dry out for several years before felling. Then they can be floated down river to the ports.

Tectona grandis
Teak

Terminalia catappa
Coast Almond, fruit

TERMINALIA

Tropical Almond,
False Kamani
* **Deciduous/fast**
* **Summer nuts**
* **Ht: to 25m/75ft**

In tropical seaside gardens and coastal areas throughout the warm-climate world, you find a curious tree much wider than it is tall! Its blunt-ended, shiny leaves are up to

143

Terminalia catappa
Coast Almond

TERMINALIA (continued)

30cm long and a few of them will be coloured a brilliant red at any time. It is in fact completely deciduous, though it tends to disguise the fact by disrobing only part at a time.

The tree is called **Terminalia catappa,** and it is valued not only for the deep shade it gives and for the sand-binding qualities of its vast root system, but also for its flattened, almond-like fruits, roasted or eaten raw.

In native cultures the reddish trunkwood is used in boat building. Very convenient, since it only grows by water!

The **Terminalia** is known by several popular names, Tropical Almond, Coast Almond and False Kamani among them.

Ternstroemia sylvatica

TERNSTROEMIA

(No popular name)
* **Evergreen /fast** C T
* **Summer berries**
* **Ht: 4-10m/12-30ft** H

Named for an eighteenth century Swedish naturalist who spent much time in China recording the native flora, **Ternstroemias** include some 45 trees and shrubs from warmer parts of Asia, Africa and tropical America. They are closely related to the **Camellia,** though the only resemblance is in the foliage.

Only two species are much cultivated: **T. sylvatica** from Mexico, and **T. gymnanthera** from Japan. Both are small trees with spirally arranged leaves, leathery and shining. Small whitish flowers are followed by summer berries.

144

THEOBROMA

Cacao, Cocoa Tree
* **Evergreen/fast**
* **Fruit year round**
* **Ht: to 12m/30ft** [H]

Food for the Gods! For once a tree's botanical name comes right to the point! Food for the Gods is what **Theobroma** means, and food for the Gods is what it gives, for the seeds of this fascinating Central American tree are the basis of every chocolate cake produced in the world!

The Cocoa Tree **Theobroma cacao** grows naturally from 5 to 12m in height, but is often trained to a lower, more branching shape to make picking easier. It is exclusively for warm climates, where it enjoys protection from sun and wind and deep, moist soil.

Theobroma cacao is evergreen, with leathery, oblong 30cm leaves, often tinted pink or red when young. The tiny, short-stemmed flowers appear at any time in dense clusters directly from the trunk or larger branches. They are yellow with a pink calyx, and are followed by purplish-brown, ten-ribbed, woody fruits which may be any size up to that of a football. These each contain about fifty flat seeds embedded in sticky white pulp.

After picking, the seeds are fermented, roasted and ground to become chocolate.

The Cocoa tree (or Cacao, to give it the Indian name) is grown from seed, and fruits at about four years of age.

Theobroma cacao
Cocoa pod

Theobroma cacao
Cocoa Tree, foliage

THUJA

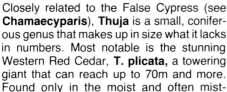

Western Red Cedar,
Arborvitae
* **Deciduous/fast** [C]
* **Foliage variation**
* **Ht: 12-70m/35-200ft** [T]

Closely related to the False Cypress (see **Chamaecyparis**), **Thuja** is a small, coniferous genus that makes up in size what it lacks in numbers. Most notable is the stunning Western Red Cedar, **T. plicata,** a towering giant that can reach up to 70m and more. Found only in the moist and often mist-shrouded coastal ranges of the Rocky

Thuja plicata
Western Red Cedar

THUJA (continued)

Mountains from California to Alaska, it is one of the world's great timber trees, source of an important softwood for internal home construction.

The Red Cedar's bark is deeply fissured, the scaly leaves arranged in flattened, horizontal branchlets. And how strange that such a big tree has such small cones! They are its trademark and are unique — the cone-scales are all hinged so that they open like a flower when ripe!

From the other side of North America comes the White Cedar, **T. occidentalis,** a tree only one-third the size, but equally valued for its timber. More popular in garden use, it is genetically unstable and has produced innumerable cultivars, varying from the parent in both colour and habit.

Across the North Pacific, the only three other species are found. These are: **T. koraiensis** from Korea; **T. orientalis,** the Chinese Arborvitae; and **T. standishii,** the Japanese Arborvitae. All are much smaller trees and popular in horticultural use. Only the Chinese species shares the colour instability.

Thujas grow slowly, and the major species may be propagated from the fine seed.

Thuja CV 'Stoneham Gold'
Golden Cedar

Thuja occidentalis
White Cedar

TILIA

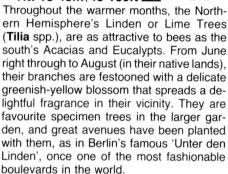

Linden, Lime
* **Deciduous**/fast C
* **Autumn colour**
* **Ht: 15-45m/45-150ft** T

Throughout the warmer months, the Northern Hemisphere's Linden or Lime Trees (**Tilia** spp.), are as attractive to bees as the south's Acacias and Eucalypts. From June right through to August (in their native lands), their branches are festooned with a delicate greenish-yellow blossom that spreads a delightful fragrance in their vicinity. They are favourite specimen trees in the larger garden, and great avenues have been planted with them, as in Berlin's famous 'Unter den Linden', once one of the most fashionable boulevards in the world.

There are about thirty species of Linden, with representative members in temperate zones of Europe, Asia and North America. They are deciduous, generally tall, with some species growing to 50m. The trunks are heavily buttressed and surrounded by suckers. The leaves are almost perfectly heart-shaped and slightly serrated, borne on long stems. The flowers are five-petalled and appear in long-stalked clusters from a showy greenish-white bract. They are followed by small, green fruits.

Limewood has been a favourite with European wood carvers from time immemorial. Pale and easily worked, it is found in more religious statues and baroque extravaganzas than any other timber, and has also been used for many practical items such as piano keys, clogs and venetian blinds.

All Linden species grow fast and well in a wide variety of soil conditions, but must have plenty of water. They are propagated from seed, layers or cuttings.

The many popular species include: **T. americana,** the American Linden or Basswood, growing to 45m, with faintly furry fruit; **T. cordata,** the European Small-leafed Linden, and its hybrid **T. X europaea,** both growing from 35 to 40m and with lightly-ribbed fruit; the American **T. heterophylla** or White Basswood; the Japanese Linden, **T. japonica** (syn. **T. miqueliena**), which grows slowly to 15m; **T. petiolaris,** the Pendant Silver Lime from south-east Europe which reaches 25m, has round, warty fruit and blossom that is particularly fragrant; **T.**

Tilia cordata
Small-leafed Lime

Tilia miqueliana
Japanese Linden

Tilia platyphyllos aurea
Gold-leaf Lime

Tilia petiolaris
Pendant Silver Lime

Tilia X europea
Common Lime

TILIA (continued)

platyphyllos, the Large-leafed Lime from Europe, 45m with 5-ribbed pea-shaped fruit; China is home to **T. tomentosa,** the Silver Lime.

Young lime foliage is a delicate chartreuse green, and older leaves of many species are silvered with fine hairs.

Tilia is the original Latin name — the French call the tree *tilleul*. Both English and German popular names Lime and Linden come from the old German *Lind*.

In earlier times, the trees were favourites of the Slavic and Germanic peoples, being planted by the wells at the centre of every town. One famous tree with a trunk diameter of 3m gave its name to the South German town Neuenstadt an der grossen Linden — Newtown by the Big Lime Tree!

148

Toona australis
Australian Red Cedar

TOONA

Red Cedar
* **Deciduous /fast**   [T]
* **Autumn colour**
* **Ht: to 30m /95ft**   [H]

Once the glory of Australia's east coastal forests, the Red Cedar or **Toona australis** is now quite rare. Throughout the nineteenth century it was mercilessly hunted out and felled without a thought for the morrow.

Australian Cedar is a softwood, beautifully grained and coloured. Wonder of wonders, it is also termite resistant!

The **Toona** tree itself is quite a curiosity — not a real Cedar of course, for Cedars are conifers, but a relative of the Chinese **Cedrelas,** and completely deciduous. The leaves are compound, with up to eight pairs of pointed leaflets, and often coloured a delicate bronze-pink when young.

The tree itself has been known to reach 70m in the wild, but is slow-growing. Today you'd have to go deep into the coastal ranges to find one of any size, though there are some fine specimens as street trees in the Northern Rivers township of Bellingen, in New South Wales. To see them in the mass, you'd need to visit Hawaii, where they have been used in reafforestation.

Toona is propagated from seed, grows fast and tall only in a subtropical climate.

Tristania conferta
Brush Box

TRISTANIA

Water Gum, Kanooka,
Brush Box
* **Evergreen/fast**
* **Decorative bark/
  foliage**
* **Ht: 6-50m/18-160ft**

T H

Named for an all-but-forgotten French
botanist, Jules Tristan, the handsome **Tris-
tanias** are a small genus found in
Australia, New Caledonia and India. Only
four are of any interest to the gardener, by far
the most important being the Australian
Brush Box, **Tristania conferta,** grown in
many lands.

A good-natured giant with lofty, reddish
trunk and branches, it may reach 40m in a
warm, moist climate, but is rather prone to
frost damage when young.

The glossy, simple leaves may reach
15cm and are carried alternately. The flowers, borne profusely among new foliage in
late spring, are creamy-white and fragrant,
with masses of feathery stamens. They are

150

TRISTANIA (continued)

followed by round seed pods, rather like the gumnuts borne by related Eucalypts. These hang on the branches all year.

Although **Tristania** is native to moist coastal forests and grows fast when young, it is surprisingly resistant to dry conditions, and has become very popular as a street tree in Australian cities. There, in a lopped, spreading shape, it is only a shadow of its tall free-growing forest cousins. There is a beautifully variegated form, **T.c. aurea variegata,** most eyecatching against a dark background.

Second in popularity is the Australian Water Gum or Kanooka, **T. laurina.** This is a much smaller tree, rarely 20m in nature, usually about 5m in cultivation. Similar in most respects to the Brush Box, its leaves are narrower and darker; the smaller flowers are noted for their golden colour rather than their fragrance. As its popular name suggests, it is a water-loving tree, and found wild along damp river banks of eastern Australia.

T. neriifolia (also called the Water Gum) is another even smaller tree for moist places; rarely reaches 6m in height.

Brush Box timber is a popular hardwood.

Tristania CV 'Aurea Variegata'
Variegated Brush Box

TSUGA

Hemlock
* **Evergreen/slow**
* **Decorative foliage**
* **Ht: 25-70m/75-230ft**

C

T

Among the crowded ranks of Northern Hemisphere conifers, the Hemlocks or **Tsuga** hold a unique, if negative place. They are not found naturally anywhere in Europe! All ten species are native to North America and eastern Asia. **Tsuga** has been the Japanese name for several thousand years.

Hemlocks are generally slow-growing and have become favourite specimen trees in cool-climate gardens with acid woodsy soil. **T. canadensis,** the Eastern Hemlock, is most commonly seen, and has produced many attractive cultivars. Among these is **T.c.** 'Pendula', with weeping branches and fine bluish foliage.

Hemlocks are quite frost-hardy and are propagated from the winged weeds of the small female cones.

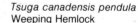

Tsuga canadensis pendula
Weeping Hemlock

Ulmus procera
English Elm

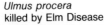
Ulmus procera
killed by Elm Disease

ULMUS

Elm
* **Deciduous/fast** [C]
* **Autumn colour**
* **Ht: 25-50m/80-160ft** [T]

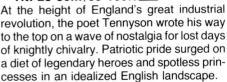

At the height of England's great industrial revolution, the poet Tennyson wrote his way to the top on a wave of nostalgia for lost days of knightly chivalry. Patriotic pride surged on a diet of legendary heroes and spotless princesses in an idealized English landscape.

Today, alas, it is the landscape itself that must provoke the deep nostalgia, for Tennyson's 'immemorial elms', the picturesque giants of English field and hedgerow, are gone — perhaps never to return — victims of a terminal disease. Weakened by the drought of 1975-76, these monarchs of the landscape were easy prey for a fungus, *Ceratocystis ulmi,* which destroys the trees' sap system.

An individual small tree might be saved by injection and spraying. Some have been, but the very size of the mature English Elms (**Ulmus procera**) was against them from the start. Trees planted in the seventeenth century had grown to 40 or 50m, and there was no way to treat them short of axe and fire. Fortunately, they have survived in the distant Southern Hemisphere, and fungus-resistant species will be planted to fill the gaps.

There are more than fifteen natural Elm species found around the temperate Northern Hemisphere in Europe, Asia and the eastern parts of North America, where they are the most favoured trees for shade and shelter, both as street trees and in lawns. They are all deciduous, and mostly tall-growing, with one curious feature that makes them easy to identify as a genus: their generally rough-textured, toothed leaves are quite asymmetrical.

Elms flower very early in the spring, in a fuzz of tiny, red-stemmed, petal-less blossom which is rarely noticed, but develops rapidly into a mass of single-seeded winged fruit, or samaras, of a delicate whitish-green.

Elms are grown easily from seed (except for the English **U. procera,** which is sterile), also from cuttings and the masses of suckers which appear around the trunks of many species. The preferred modern method is to graft these onto stock of sucker-free types.

Other commonly grown Elm species in-

Ulmus X *hollandica*
Dutch Elm

Ulmus glabra pendula
Weeping Scotch Elm

Ulmus procera
seed detail

ULMUS (continued)

clude American White Elm, **U. americana,** a
fine tree of 30m immortalized in so many
movies of American small-town life. It has
long, slender leaves that colour a brilliant
yellow in autumn, and a spreading crown with
weeping branches. The Slippery Elm **(U.
fulva),** a smaller, less common American
species grows to 25m; the leaves are long
and finely pointed, the seeds bear a patch of
red-brown hair. The Wych or Scotch Elm **(U.
glabra)** is a 40m giant in northern Europe,
but most often seen in its smaller garden
form, **U. glabra pendula,** the Weeping Elm.
This has rigidly downward-pointing branches
and is grafted on a tall stock. The rough-
textured leaves are deeply veined and oval,
and appear with the fruit. **U.** X **hollandica,**
the Dutch Elm, is believed to be a natural
hybrid of several European species. It is a
very large tree, usually with weeping outer

Ulmus parvifolia
Chinese Elm

Xanthoxylum americanum
Prickly Ash

ULMUS (continued)

branches, and inclined to sucker badly. Its autumn colour is very rich. The Chinese Elm, **U. parvifolia,** is a much smaller tree all round. Very rarely exceeding 15m, it has delightfully mottled bark and heavily weeping branches. Enjoying a warmer climate, its leaves are rarely above 2.5cm long, perfect miniatures of the full-size Elm foliage. Its crop of showy seeds is borne in autumn.

U. procera has several decorative varieties which are favourites in disease-free areas. These include the small **U.p.** 'Vanhouttei' with large golden yellow leaves all year, and **U.p.** 'Variegata', the Silver Elm, a much larger tree with variegated leaves.

In the United States, **U. thomasii,** the Rock Elm, is also seen; tall grower, it has a vertical shape, downy buds, long double-toothed leaves with flowers in racemes.

Timber of many Elm species (generally a pale, light gold) has been used in the making of country furniture.

XANTHOXYLUM

(syn. ZANTHOXYLUM)

Toothache Tree,
Prickly Ash
* **Deciduous /fast** T
* **Summer berries** C
* **Ht: to 8m /25ft**

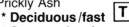

This small, slender tree from the eastern United States and Canada is grown in many cool and temperate areas of the world for its decorative value most of the year.

Xanthoxylum americanum is its name, and the mildly prickly branches open the spring season with small clusters of greenish-yellow flowers, borne in the axils of the deciduous leaves. These are handsome, compound and up to 30cm in length, each consisting of 5-11 leaflets, very much in the style of an Ash tree (see **Fraxinus**). Small berries develop after the flowers, gradually ripening to a rich red in late summer, and remaining on the tree after leaf fall. Both the berries and the leaves have mildly medicinal qualities, which presumably have a bearing on its popular epithet 'Toothache Tree'.

Zizyphus mauritiana
Indian Jujube

ZIZYPHUS

Jujube Tree, Chinese Date
* **Deciduous/evergreen/
  fast growing**
* **Winter fruits**
* **Ht: 10-13m/30-40ft** [T] [H]

The Jujubes are native mostly to warm temperate areas of the Northern Hemisphere. Their curious botanical name is from the original Arabic name *zizouf*.

Most commonly grown by far is **Z. jujuba,** the Chinese Date or Common Jujube, a deciduous 13m tree found right across Asia. The fleshy, juicy, orange-red fruits, which ripen in late winter, are a great favourite in the Arabic countries, where they are preserved and dried and made into many sticky confections — presumably the origin of our own jujube candies. The leaves are oblong-elliptic in shape and up to 5cm long, lightly spined on the stem.

Closely related **Z. mauritiana** or Indian Jujube is similar, though usually smaller-growing and evergreen. The fruits are quite acid and need stewing with sugar. It is a round-headed to shrubby tree, with more heavily spined leaf stems.

According to legend, **Z. spina-christi** from north Africa and Asia Minor was the tree from which Christ's Crown of Thorns was woven. It grows to 10m only, is a sparsely-branched, shrubby plant with viciously spined leaf stems. It bears grape-sized fruits which are quite edible, but should be picked with great care. Propagated from seed or cuttings.

INDEX

All popular names and synonyms used anywhere in this book are listed here in alphabetical order, with cross reference to the botanical genus under which the plants are arranged throughout the text. Botanical generic names are also listed. Species, named colour varieties, cultivars and illustrations will be found within these alphabetically arranged entries.

160